GETTING
REAL

**CORWIN
PRESS**

GETTING
REAL

Helping Teens
Find Their Future

Kenneth Gray

CORWIN PRESS, INC.
A Sage Publications Company
Thousand Oaks, California

For information address:

CORWIN
PRESS

Corwin Press, Inc.
A Sage Publications Company
2455 Teller Road
Thousand Oaks, California 91320
E-mail: order@corwinpress.com

SAGE Publications Ltd.
6 Bonhill Street
London EC2A 4PU
United Kingdom

SAGE Publications India Pvt. Ltd.
M-32 Market
Greater Kailash I
New Delhi 110 048 India

Printed in the United States of America

Library of Congress Cataloging-in-Publication Data

Gray, Kenneth C.
  Getting Real: Helping teens find their future/
by Kenneth Gray.
    p. cm.
  Includes bibliographical references.
  ISBN 0-7619-7514-4 (cloth: alk. paper)
  ISBN 0-7619-7515-2 (paper: alk. paper)
    1. Vocational guidance—United States. 2. High school graduates—Employment—United States. 3. High school students—Vocational guidance—United States. 4. Postsecondary education—United States. I. Title.
  HF5382.5 U5 G676 1999
  331.7′0233—dc21   99-6181

This book is printed on acid-free paper.

                        04 05 06 7 6

Editorial Assistant: Julia Parnell
Production Editor: Denise Santoyo
Editorial Assistant: Patricia Zeman
Typesetter/Designer: Marion Warren
Indexer: Teri Greenberg
Cover Designer: Candice Harman

Contents

Preface

In my youth, teens jarred their friends back to reality with the phrase "dream on"; now, they say "get real." At least when it comes to postsecondary planning, many teens would benefit from taking such advice. Because of poor planning or no planning at all, most teens head off to college—ready or not—and, predictably, most fail. Either they drop out or not; if they do not, they fail to find commensurate employment. The overall purpose of this book is to improve the odds. It is time to stop taking pride in how many teens go to college and start asking instead how many teens are successful—epecially, how many matriculate without the need for remedial college courses, graduate on time, and find commensurate employment?

Postsecondary success hinges on two factors: academic skills and commitment that comes from career direction. This statement is not opinion, but rather is based on research findings. Whereas academic maturity has long been a priority of the schools and the nation, career maturity has not. This attitude must change. Poor academic skills and lack of career focus both predict postsecondary failure.

This book has two specific purposes: (a) to illuminate the quiet dilemma in the United States that stems from a mismatch between teens' aspirations and the economic/labor market realities they will face as adults and (b) to guide educators, parents, employers, elected officials, and anyone else who is interested in helping teens develop career direction and thus make better postsecondary decisions. The overall goal is to stimulate efforts designed to develop a level of maturity—termed *career maturity* or *career direction*—among teens that allows them to make postsecondary plans that have a high probability of success.

This book is a sequel to the book *Other Ways to Win* (Gray & Herr, 1995), which argued that most teens have concluded that there is now only "one way to win"—namely, get a 4-year college degree. The results of this strategy have not changed. At least for those in the academic middle, it leads to failure and disappointment with almost mathematical predictability. Fortunately, however, there are "other ways to win"—specifically, in the areas of high-skill/high-wage technical careers that may require higher education but not a 4-year degree.

After 5 years of speaking around the country and conducting further research, I have concluded that these "other ways to win" are largely ignored because many teens and their parents do not consider alternatives to a 4-year degree. In fact, many teens do not plan at all: For them, college is a default decision; not knowing what to do, they go to college and then fail. This must change if the goal is postsecondary success. Parents and teens need help in making better postsecondary decisions; only then will the "one way to win" mentality diminish.

Teenagers are not entirely to blame; conventional wisdom actually works to downplay, if not discourage, career decisions. Furthermore, overexpansion in higher education has removed all barriers to admissions, including ability to do college-level academics. Thus, I have concluded that those who could benefit from considering "other ways to win" will not do so until they have been helped to become better decisions makers, more focused, and more willing to face reality. This book is for those who would help them reach this plateau. This goal is relevant for all teenagers, including the academically blessed. Lack of career direction predicts failure for good students just as much as it does for the less blessed.

Following an introductory chapter on the current state of "unreality" among today's youths, this book is divided into two parts. Part 1 provides background information necessary for career development efforts. Chapter 2 discusses labor market realities this generation of teens will face and exposes the folly of several pervasive but harmful pieces of advice given to teens about career decision making. Chapter 3 provides details regarding career opportunities, and

Chapter 4 discusses the importance of countering occupational stereotypes that tend to limit opportunity for women and the disadvantaged. The chapters in Part 2 provide detailed information and strategies for developing career development programs. Chapter 5 outlines tactics to foster career maturity among today's youths, Chapter 6 discusses various postsecondary alternatives for teens, and Chapter 7 provides specific messages for talking to parents and the business community. Included in Chapter 7 is a presentation for parents called a "REAL" plan for postsecondary success. The final chapter (8) presents a summary of the issues, beginning with a discussion of the wisdom of continuing the practice of giving youths a steady diet of "nutritional lies."

As an introduction to Chapter 1, it is worth observing that the importance of the three academic "R's"—reading, 'riting, and 'rithmetic—is well understood. Not well understood at all is that, for this generation, a fourth "R" is needed; this "R" stands for the willingness to deal with *reality*. It is easy for teens and parents to postpone dealing with reality: Open-door college admissions and student loans based on need, not academic readiness, make it all too easy. Sooner or later, however, reality calls. Very few beat the odds, and the odds are not good. Failure to deal with reality predicts failure. I hope this book promotes success by helping teens "get real" and, by so doing, improve their individual odds of success.

Acknowledgments

Many individuals made this book possible, beginning with Alice Foster of Corwin Press, who urged me to write it, and all those in the audiences across the country who wanted to know when the "next book" would be out. Special thanks to my mentor, Ed Herr; my assistant, Tammy Fetterolf; my editor, Lee Carpenter, who always makes my work a lot better; and those who reviewed the first draft. The contributions of the following reviewers are also gratefully acknowledged: Dr. Lynn Erickson, consultant and author on curriculum design, Lynn Erickson Educational Consulting, Mill Creek, Washington; Dr. Colleen Thoma, College of Education, University of Nevada, Las Vegas; and Ron Wahlen, third-grade classroom teacher, Conn Global Communications Magnet Elementary School, Raleigh, North Carolina.

About the Author

Kenneth Gray is Professor of Education in the Workforce Education and Development Program, College of Education, Penn State University. He holds a BA in Economics from Colby College, an MA in Counseling Psychology from Syracuse University, and an EdD in Vocational Technical Education from Virginia Tech. Prior to joining the faculty at Penn State in 1987, he was the Superintendent of Schools for the Connecticut Vocational Technical High School System. He has also been a high school English teacher, guidance counselor, administrator, and coach. The principal author of *Other Ways to Win: Creating Alternatives for High School Graduates* and coauthor of *Workforce Education: The Basics,* he is frequently quoted in the national press and widely published on topics regarding alternatives to bachelor's degree education for teens. He is recognized as a national advocate for students from the academic middle and postsecondary pre-bachelor's degree technical education and speaks nationally and internationally on these topics.

*To my mother Mary
and her friend Barbara*

Chapter 1

Getting Real

New Realities for Postsecondary Success

Agencies, schools, governments, and researchers have spent a lot of time counting and speaking positively about the number of teens who go on to college. It's time to move on. Virtually all barriers to college, including academic ability, have been removed for most young Americans. In the meantime, the fixation on enrollment masks a dark truth: Most teenagers who attempt college fail either by not graduating or by not finding commensurate employment if they do. It's time to move from promoting postsecondary admissions to promoting postsecondary success, be it in university education, pre-bachelor's degree technical education, work, or other pursuits. For those who go on to postsecondary education, which will be the majority, *success* is defined in this book as matriculating without the need for remedial college courses, graduating on time, and then finding employment that is commensurate with the level and type of education pursued.

Postsecondary success, as defined above, requires two ingredients: academic skills and commitment that comes from career focus. Whereas the former has been the traditional focus of the schools, the latter has not. This must change. Going to college without the commitment that stems from a clearly laid-out plan will invariably lead to failure. Past generations were schooled according to the three

1

"R's": reading, 'riting, and 'rithmetic. For this generation, a fourth "R"—*reality*—has become as important. Success comes from effective postsecondary planning that is based on reality. The purpose of this book is to guide those who would promote postsecondary success for this generation by helping teens "get real."

The Quiet Dilemma

If paradoxes count, the turn of the 20th century toward the 21st is promising to be an interesting time for teens, parents, and employers. First, despite evidence that only 40% of the nation's teens graduate from high school with the academic skills needed to do college-level work, the percentage attempting college at public expense is growing steadily. The U.S. Bureau of Labor Statistics reported that, of the 2.8 million teens who graduated from high school in 1997, 67% were enrolled in college the following October (U.S. Department of Labor, 1998a); within 2 years of graduation, 72% were enrolled. But while college enrollments grow, so do college remedial education and dropout rates. By the late 1990s, college dropout rates were at record levels. Two thirds of all college students now withdraw at least once before finishing, and 91% of these never earn a degree.

Second, although teens said the main reason they were going to college was to get a good job (American Council on Education, 1998), very few seem to have thought much about the details. Many end up completing degrees that lead to few opportunities. Of the 67% of the high school class of 1997 who enrolled in higher education immediately after graduation, two thirds matriculated in 4-year colleges to earn bachelor's degrees, but only 23% of all employment requires this level of education. Thus, by the mid-1990s at least one in three university graduates was underemployed, while in professional occupations, such as teaching, engineering, and marketing, the ratio was one in two.

Third, while increasing numbers of college graduates were ending up in low-wage service jobs, the nation's economy was generating record numbers of unfilled positions for technicians in high-skill/high-wage technical jobs. The problem was not an undersupply of college graduates, but rather an undersupply of technically skilled graduates. Companies complained of being forced to turn down contracts because of the lack of skilled workers and asked Congress to increase the number of technically skilled foreign workers they could recruit from other countries using H1-B visas, which it did in October 1998.

Fourth, on discovering they had made a mistake, many young adults became "reverse transfers," enrolling in 1- and 2-year technical programs at community and technical colleges even though many already had 4-year degrees and even graduate degrees. Why? They hoped it would give them what their bachelor's degrees had not—an advantage in competing for high-skill/high-wage employment.

Clearly, these young Americans made bad decisions. The facts suggest that most teens are still making bad decisions. In fact, many high school graduates do not make any decisions at all: College has become a default decision. Unfortunately, for these students, it's also a wasteful one, as well as expensive to teens, their parents, and the public, who foot all or part of the bill. And this situation is not benign. Failure does not build confidence or character.

Without intervention, this wasteful, harmful fiasco will continue as long as teens and parents make postsecondary plans that ignore reality. It will continue as long as the focus is on college, not on success.

A New Goal: Postsecondary Success

Increasing the number of college admissions is the unquestioned priority of the nation, its states, and local school boards as well. The supreme benchmark of the effectiveness of local school systems is the number of their teens who go on to college, not academic achievement or workplace readiness. This is indicated by the fact that the federal government spends $40 billion annually on student financial aid and the states spend another $3 billion. Some states include additional incentives, such as state-sponsored college saving programs for parents: In Georgia, a B average in high school now ensures a free college education at a state institution.

Polls indicate that the public thinks all students who have the talent and motivation to attend college should be able to go. By the mid-1990s, it was time to declare victory. In 1995, 62% of all graduating seniors were enrolled in college the October following graduation (U.S. Department of Education, 1997). Another 10% waited a year. Within 2 years of graduation, 72% had enrolled. Celebrating, however, was premature.

College Dropouts

By the mid-1990s, virtually all barriers to higher education had been removed, including ability to do college-level academics. Of the 3,842 degree-granting higher education institutions in the United States, all but several hundred "medallion" colleges and universities practice open admissions, taking 70% or more of those who apply. Estimates on the number of teens who end up in noncredit college remedial courses range from 30% to 80%, depending on the institution. As college matriculation rates have increased, so, too, have dropout rates. Let's take 2-year public higher education institutions as an example: 100% of these offer remedial courses, 41% of students are enrolled in these courses, and the first-year dropout rate is 43% (U.S. Department of Education, 1997). The current 6-year graduation rate at 4-year colleges is around 52%. Taking the class of 1990 as an example, of the 60% who went on directly after high school, only 34% had earned either an associate or a bachelor's degree 4 years later. Even though some of these students may ultimately obtain degrees sometime in the future, the reality is that, among teens who try college, at best only half have finished 6 years later. The conclusion is obvious: In terms of persisting to graduation, college means failure, not success, for at least one in two students. But disappointment awaits many of those who do graduate.

Underemployed College Graduates

Considering that most teens enter college thinking it will pay off in the labor market, success for the college-bound must include both graduating and successfully competing for commensurate college-level employment. Most teens and parents maintain that a college degree is a ticket to a college-level job. Although this was true for past generations, it is not now. The reality is that at least one in three 4-year college graduates will end up taking a job he or she could have gotten right out of high school; by 2005, it will be close to one in two. Except for those who graduate with college degrees that will fit with the sought-after skills in high demand, a 4-year college degree today is only a ticket to get in line for college-level employment. Unfortunately, more graduates are in line than opportunities are available. Instead of being a ticket to opportunity, a college degree is more like a ticket on an oversold flight on a holiday weekend. More shocking still—at least to parents—is that many graduates end up filling out applications at the local mall and moving back home. For them, college did not result in success even though they graduated.

In the light of these realities, it's time to set new goals for teens and the institutions that prepare them. The goal is not college; most who try college fail. If we add the number of those who do not graduate from college with the number who do but are underemployed, the success rate is, at best, one in three—not very good. A new goal is needed. That goal should be postsecondary success.

> Every student will graduate from high school having developed a postsecondary plan that has a high probability of success.

The new benchmark should be how graduates fare the first year after high school. A postsecondary plan with a high probability of success for some youths will be matriculation at a university, but for many others, alternatives need to be considered, particularly pre-bachelor's degree technical education or even taking a year off, or a prep year, before enrolling.

Success rates will increase only when students and parents start making better decisions that are based on thought-out career directions and a consideration of all alternatives, including a university. Making such decisions requires career direction. For this generation, the number one predictor of postsecondary success, particularly in college, is not grades (today, it is all but impossible to flunk out of college), but rather having a goal or the commitment that comes from career maturity and career direction (Cope & Hannah, 1975).

Career Maturity and Career Direction

Parents, teachers, and even most teens recognize the nexuses between academic skills, as indicated by grades, and college entrance exams and college admissions. Of students with a C average in high school who enroll in a 4-year college, only 8% complete a bachelor's degree, compared with 54% of those with an A average (Astin & Dey, 1989). It should be noted, however, that many students with good high school grades and test scores also drop out of college. Although students with a combined SAT score of 1,300 or higher are five times more likely to graduate from college than those with a 700, the surprising thing is that only two thirds of the academically blessed graduate. Academically, these students are obviously all dressed up and ready to go, but if they do go and graduate, all too many end up underemployed.

Success in college depends on many factors, one of which is academic ability. The research of Tinto (1993), Bean and Metzner (1996), and others on why students leave college provides some answers. Students leave for four main reasons: (a) poor academic skills, (b) lack of money, (c) feelings of alienation at college, and (d) lack of commitment that accompanies lack of a clear goal or reason for sticking it out. Of the variables associated with lack of persistence, lack of focus or commitment is too often overlooked, but is the most important.

The importance of commitment or focus in predicting persistence is illustrated by noting the time when students are the most likely to drop out of college. Many never survive the freshman year. Nationally, 27% of matriculating college students drop out then. Subtracting those who leave between semesters, about one third of the rest depart in the first 3 weeks of the first semester. Considering that, in many large universities, it may take that long just to find classes, it is clear that these students did not want to be in college in the first place; their commitment was zero. Importantly, some of these students are among the most academically qualified.

Another common time for students to leave is between the sophomore and junior years. Although most college students can hang around and take courses forever, to get a degree a student must eventually choose a major. For many, this is the moment of truth. They had no specific interest when they enrolled, and 2 years later they are still clueless. Facing mounting student loan debt and little motivation, many simply leave. Others stick around and engage in a new pastime known as "major of the month." These students change college academic majors frequently—one reason why the average time to graduate from a public 4-year college is now more than 5 years.

Although changing a major can be a sign of developing a career focus, changing majors frequently and randomly is not. Changing majors is not benign either. At most universities, changing a major means another year, which increases both the cost and time for a degree. For most students who change majors, graduation means underemployment. They entered college not knowing where they were headed, and they graduated the same way. In the end, they chose a major that was the quickest or easiest route to getting out with a degree. They would have been wise to heed the advice contained in *Workforce 2020* (Judy & D'Amico, 1997):

> Simply getting a college degree, regardless of major, will not be all that helpful for those entering the twenty-first century workplace. The specific field of study matters a great deal—far more than simply getting a diploma. Students should focus their energies acquiring the specific skills and kinds of knowledge demanded by occupations that are both growing rapidly and paying well. (p. 69)

Had many of today's college graduates heeded this advice in the first place, they would have graduated dressed up and with somewhere to go. Likewise, many who dropped out would have persisted to graduation. In a study of community college students, for example, Kostelba (1997) found that those who enrolled in occupation-specific programs—indicating a specific career interest and thus a reason for attending—were statistically more likely to graduate. These students knew why they had enrolled. They had achieved an appropriate level of career maturity.

Defining Career Maturity

What do I mean by career maturity? Like all forms of maturity, what is considered mature behavior for a 7-year-old differs from that considered mature for an 18-year-old. Career fantasy, unencumbered by reality, is natural and desirable in the elementary grades, but by the junior year of high school, such fantasy is a sign of career immaturity. Such maturity is demonstrated by teenagers of high school age when they

1. Understand the importance of narrowing career interests as a basis for postsecondary planning
2. Have, by the 10th grade, identified one or more career interests after an objective evaluation of their likes and dislikes, their aptitudes, and labor market projections

3. Have, by the end of the 12th grade, engaged in activities to verify these choices
4. Used these choices to make post-high-school decisions

This operational definition of career maturity suggests that high school seniors should exhibit four characteristics upon graduation:

1. They should understand that career direction, even a tentative one, is as important to developing postsecondary success as good grades.
2. They should have made tentative choices by the 10th grade.
3. They should have taken actions that would verify these choices during their final 2 years of high school.
4. They should use these decisions as one focus for postsecondary planning.

The idea is simple and old-fashioned. Deciding what to do after high school should be based on a realistic personal assessment of individual likes and dislikes, as well as strengths and weaknesses as they relate to labor market opportunities; making career decisions; and then exploring alternatives to prepare to pursue these interests. Perhaps most important is the attitude implied by these behaviors: that success comes from planning and that planning requires knowing the direction in which one wants to head. Today, many teens take a far different view. They go to college and sit back and see what will happen when it is over. Many do not have to wait very long. Lacking any commitment, they soon leave. This is true even among the academically blessed.

Students who start college intending to major in engineering is a good example. Among entering freshmen who intend to major in engineering, many change their minds quickly. For example, at one major engineering college, 50% of women and 40% of men dropped the major during their freshman year. What's the reason for the high rate? Students admitted to engineering are always among the most academically blessed on campus. For many, the problem is not the academics, but rather that they had no idea what they were getting into or what they really wanted in the first place. In most cases, they elected engineering solely on the advice of others, without making any effort to find out what a practicing engineer does and thus whether they would like it. The typical advice to teens who are blessed with academic ability in mathematics and science but who have no career focus is to major in engineering. Many follow the advice without making any effort to verify whether they would like this type of work and thus do not make a real commitment. When they finally get started in their engineering major—sometimes not until the junior year in college—they discover a little late that it's not for them. Although they may have been academically mature, they exhibited all the signs of career immaturity.

Notice that, among teens, developing career maturity does not mean forcing them to make decisions at age 18 on the "one best" career for them or—to use the conventional wisdom—locking them into this decision. The hope is that much of the narrowing down process will take place during the high school years and not while incurring great expense in college or enduring disappointments in the labor market. Many teens will change their minds later, but if they make good decisions in the first place, their new interests should relate to the originals. Also, many teens will find it impossible to narrow their interests and choices to just one career focus. If so, some logical nexuses between these multiple career interests are necessary.

A high school senior who expresses an interest in both computer-aided manufacturing and computer graphic design and makes postsecondary plans accordingly is exhibiting career maturity. A high school senior who expresses an interest in being either an astronaut or a tattoo artist may need some assistance. Why? Because there are significant occupational similarities between computer-aided manufacturing and computer graphic design, but there are none between astronaut and tattoo artist.

Rethinking Our Attitude Toward Career Decision Making

The hopes and dreams of many of today's youths are hopelessly out of sync with their aptitudes and other realities. Beyond a vague notion of wanting a good job in order to make a decent living, many teens have few specific hopes and dreams. This is not totally their fault, however. Until now, the conventional wisdom has been that the lack of career focus among teens not only is normal but may be desirable.

It is interesting to observe that whereas lack of academic maturity—meaning poor skills and thus poor grades—is generally considered cause for concern, lack of commitment stemming from career focus is not. For example, a teacher, counselor, or parent may sense trouble ahead for a high school senior who is planning to go to college but has yet to pass the first level of algebra. But no such reservations are expressed about A-average students who do not know why they are going to college. This double standard seems to be rooted in outdated notions about the labor market this generation will face and in outdated beliefs about the danger of making career decisions. Two old "saws" illustrate these attitudes. The first is "Be careful about making career decisions too early; you don't want to close any doors." The second is "Don't panic if you have no career interests; you will decide that in college." As is discussed in later chapters, both are terrible pieces of advice to give today's teens. Suffice it to say for now that, for this generation, a lack of commitment predicts failure in higher education, and career focus is the best source of such commitment. This book is predicated on one main thesis.

> For this generation, career maturity is as important as academic maturity. Both predict post-high-school success.

The Role of Adults and the Community in Teenage Career Development

Although most people would agree that schools are responsible for instilling academic maturity among the college bound, they are uncertain about who or what is responsible for career maturity. For example, some believe that the best way for a teenager to maximize his or her opportunities is to postpone any career decision as long as possible—go to college and see what happens afterward. Others worry that making students deal with the reality will discourage them. Not wanting to "step on teenagers' dreams," they prefer to keep quiet and let the teens drift. Thus, the focus is on getting students into college, not on facing what will happen after they get there.

Still others (sometimes for historically sound reasons) see a plot afoot. To them, career exploration in any form is simply a new "code word" for social engineering. They point out, accurately, that students from impoverished homes are already the least likely to attend college and the most likely to end up in low-paying jobs. Even though *career exploration* may be the preferred term, they believe that more "persuasion" than "exploration" is going on, that teenagers are being told what they can and cannot do. Along the same lines, some view efforts to assist teens in developing career maturity as an infringement on family rights; the attitude is that schools should stick to academics while parents tell their children what to do after high school graduation.

Added to these concerns is the thorny issue of "false negatives." The fact is that some people beat the odds, and it is virtually impossible to predict who those will be. A few individuals succeed when all objective data would suggest otherwise. In fact, those who do are like folk heroes: They personify the American dream. Had they made logical decisions and not tried, they would not have succeeded. Knowledge of those who beat the odds seems to devalue the importance of objective planning.

While recognizing the sincerity and evidence for all these views, we are obligated to think about the alternative that we as a nation have chosen and its results. Because we do not want to discourage youths, because we worry about unequal effects, and because we remember those who beat the odds, policymakers have created a higher education capacity that can accommodate everyone and thus allow all to avoid reality—but only for a short time.

Higher Education/Labor Market Darwinism

Little attention is paid to what may be the real function of higher education in the United States. It is not creating opportunity: Honest numbers suggest that as few as one third ever graduate from college and end up with commensurate employment and that these tend to be the children of the upper middle class. Nor is it the transmission of culture; television and other mass media, not universities, now are the preservers and transmitters of culture. What, then, is the real function of higher education? One thing higher education does very well is society's dirty work: It sorts the fit from the unfit. And if the college system fails to weed out all the unfit, the labor market will finish the job in Machiavellian fashion. Although we let everyone pursue his or her fantasies in college, the majority will fail at great expense. We call it equal opportunity. It can just as well be called higher education/labor market Darwinism. What we have done, in fact, is create a system in which youths (and parents) can postpone facing reality. In the end, though, the reality comes at great expense for most.

So, what is the answer? Are creating opportunity and realistic career planning incompatible? Perhaps Herr and Cramer (1996) provide a middle ground for these differing points of view regarding teenage career decision making: "One cannot choose what one does not know about, does not know how to prepare for, or how to gain access to" (p. 126).

If the goal of democracy is individual opportunity, meaning equal access to competition for desirable employment, how can one exercise this right without knowing what the options are? As Herr and Cramer (1996) point out, one cannot prepare to compete for what one does not know about. And it should be clear that, to date, institutions of higher education have not proved to be very good places to make these sorts of determinations. Even if they were, they're one of the most expensive places in the world to do it. Teens themselves realize the importance of having career goals. In follow-up surveys of high school graduates, students with all levels of academic ability indicate a wish to have had more opportunity to explore careers in college (Gray & Huang, 1993). They look to schools for help, not necessarily to tell them what they should or should not do, but for help in making these decisions.

The Role of Public Schools

Much of the ambivalence among educators regarding career development programs revolves around confusion about their role in the programs. This confusion seems to be based on the misconception that career guidance entails educators telling teenagers what they should or should not do after graduation from high school. This is not the point at all.

Clearly, the decision regarding post-high-school plans is for students and parents to make. Schools help them be in a position, if they wish, to make informed (mature) decisions (resembling the consumerist movement in America, wherein the philosophy was that individuals have a right to be informed but that the decision is still theirs to make). For example, despite overwhelming evidence that smoking is hazardous to one's health, anyone over a certain age is free to buy cigarettes. The government's role is not to make the decision, but to provide consumers with information in the hope that they will make better, more mature decisions. Career development programs in schools are developed around the same philosophy. The point is not to make the decision for teens, but to make teens better decision makers. Why? So that more will ultimately be successful. The bottom line is that students and parents report wanting help with career decision making.

Most parents' hopes and dreams for their children include college. Given that reality, most parents also want their children to graduate and, after they do, to land college-level jobs. With this goal in mind, parents seem to be sensing the need for their children to be focused. In one representative study conducted by PBS, 93% of adults thought that providing seminars that relayed information on career options and the skills required for various careers was an appropriate role for public schools; 94% approved of school-sponsored, work-based internships ("Polls Show Support," 1998, p. 6). The widespread success of the Bring Your Daughter to Work program is another indicator of growing parental concern about the need for career focus.

Although parents understand this need, they are less and less likely to be able to do the job alone. In times past, parents' occupations were typically the dominant influence in the career interests of their teens. Not any longer. A recent Harris poll reports, for example, that 62% of entering college freshmen would not "even consider" pursuing the same career as either parent (Carey & Parker, 1998). Thus, although some family rights groups argue that setting career direction is the role of the family and not of the school, this is a minority view. Data suggest that, in fact, the family is playing a smaller and smaller role in this process, leaving nothing to take its place. This is not to say that parents are no longer important influences in teens' postsecondary plans, but they are increasingly less prepared to influence or guide career decision making. This decline in parental influence is not surprising, considering that half of all workers report being unsatisfied with their jobs and would not recommend that their children follow in their footsteps. And although the stated goal of the majority of teens is a professional career, two thirds of all adults with professional careers say they wish they had done something else. In this vacuum, parents are looking to the schools for help in developing in their teens a level of career maturity along with academic maturity.

Making the Case for Career Development Programs

Individuals who seek to promote efforts toward career maturity face many challenges, beginning with a need to convince skeptical teens and adults of its importance. Four reasons for this are provided in this section of the chapter.

Reason 1: Postsecondary Failure

The first and most important reason for career development efforts is that today more than half of all high school graduates pursue postsecondary plans that end in failure. Reviewing the numbers: 69% go directly to college; 72% enroll within 2 years of graduation, two thirds of whom enroll in 4-year colleges, but 30% or more must take remedial education; about half graduate within 6 years, and of those who do, one in two goes underemployed. Obviously, there is room for improvement.

How can the success rate be improved? Research is clear. Two things are important: academic skills and the commitment that comes from career focus.

Reason 2: The "One Way to Win" Mentality

The best evidence of the need for efforts to promote career maturity is the degree to which the nation's teens and their parents and almost everyone else have become irrationally addicted to the "one way to win" mentality. Specifically, they have concluded that the only hope for success in the future is to (a) get a 4-year degree (b) in order to obtain high-wage employment (c) in the professional ranks.

In a National Center for Educational Statistics (NCES) longitudinal survey conducted in 1990, 95% of all high school sophomores in the sample indicated expecting to go on to college, up from 78% in the 1970s. Consistently, surveys of entering college freshmen indicate that students' primary reason for attending college is to "get a better job." Setting aside the fact that only 40% of today's teens graduate from high school prepared to do college-level academics, the NCES findings reveal more cause for concern: About one half of all teens and two thirds of female teens indicate a desire to be engaged in a professional occupation when they are 30 years old. Currently and in the future, however, only 20% of all work is or will be in the professional/managerial ranks.

Survey data on the entering freshmen class of 2001 (ACES, 1998) show the same trends: 50% plan to major in managerial/professional areas, and only 4% in technical fields; unfortunately, in terms of net opportunity (see Chapters 2 and 3), managerial/professional is dead last among the six major occupational groups. It is projected that the economy will generate only about half as many jobs as graduates annually. Clearly, the hopes and dreams of more than half of all teens in these surveys are out of touch with reality. In fact, the success rate among those who try the "one way to win" strategy is, at best, one in three. One reason is poor academic skills, and a more fundamental reason is poor decision making in the first place. A lack of awareness of alternatives has led teens and their parents to make the default choice; on graduation, then, more often than not, they head off toward failure. If they knew of other alternatives, some would make better decisions and thus fewer would fail.

Reason 3: Gender and Other Occupational Stereotypes

An equally compelling reason to help teens "get real" is the continued detrimental effects of gender-specific occupational stereotyping. For a variety of complex reasons, young girls and boys do not consider certain occupations because they are nontraditional for their gender. Of particular concern is the aversion of many girls to technical, manufacturing, and skilled trade careers. These stereotypical views have detrimental effects on both individuals and the nation. For example, 35 years after the Equal Pay Act, women still earn 76 cents to the $1.00 earned by men. Meanwhile, the shortage of information technology workers that developed in the late 1990s was partially attributed to the reality that few women select this field.

Other equally pernicious occupational stereotypes persist that are race, ethics, or region specific. Such stereotypes narrow the range of opportunities that teens consider and thereby narrow their opportunities. This topic is important enough that Chapter 4 is devoted entirely to it. Suffice it to say here that "getting real" includes helping youths see beyond stereotypical views of themselves and work.

Reason 4: National Skills Shortage

The 1990s was a time of dramatic economic growth in the United States. Between 1991 and 1996, the gross domestic product (GDP) increased from $4.9 to $7.6 trillion, with an inflation rate of only 2.9%. As the end of the decade approached, however, serious labor shortages developed. The term *labor shortage* does not accurately reflect the situation, though. The shortage was not of people, but of people with skill. Be it information technology industries, precision manufacturing, electronics production, or building construction, virtually all industries that employed technical workers—workers who used math and science principles in making decisions on the job—faced shortages.

The skills shortage quickly became a national issue. The Hudson Institute (Judy & D'Amico, 1997) predicted that unless the skills gap was closed, the GDP could be negatively affected by as much as 5%. The reality of such predictions is illustrated by a study of the impact of labor shortages on one Pennsylvania county (Wall, Passmore, et al., 1996), where the inability of one firm to hire 30 precision machinists led it to curtail expansion plans, which in turn led to a countywide economic loss of $20 million in economic output and $3 million in tax revenue. Unable to fill jobs, employers turn to the Congress, asking that the number of H-1B immigration visas be increased to recruit internationally for skill workers.

How did such a skills mismatch develop? Predictably, schools, both high schools and colleges, were the first to be blamed. The general consensus was that they simply were not turning out sufficient numbers of people with the work skills needed. Such charges missed the point. The problem was not that students did not have the technical skills, but that they all wanted to be professionals. The shortage of technicians could be ascribed to the simple reality that, among those with the necessary talent, few were interested because few knew anything about such career opportunities.

Between 1985 and 1997, the number of bachelor of science degrees in engineering awarded in the United States fell 16%; computer science and mathematics degrees awarded fell 29%. Only 12% of all degrees awarded in the United States were in technical areas. But was this the fault of the nation's schools and colleges? Hardly! In the Pennsylvania county mentioned above, an existing precision manufacturing training program was on the verge of closing because of a lack of student interest. Of all PhD graduates in technical fields in the United States, 48% are foreign students; universities admit these students because U.S. youths are either not interested or unwilling to make the financial sacrifice.

The skills gap that developed in the 1990s was the result of many factors. The fundamental problem was that many poor decisions were being made by young adults. The skills gap was a predictable result of widespread career illiteracy. As argued previously, today's youths are not just making bad decisions; most are making no decisions, going to college by default at public expense as if it were just the 13th year of school (which, for many, is close to the truth).

This gap will not close until the nation's youths choose to pursue careers in areas of high technical demand. In the United States, federal and state governments have neither the power nor the will to mandate these decisions. It is up to the individual. The only hope is that teens will make better decisions when they are better informed. Thus, a logical role of government is to prepare today's youths and their parents to make better choices. The skills gap will narrow significantly only when the general level of career maturity increases. Meanwhile, efforts to increase the level of career maturity among teens will be accepted by the public only when they are helped to realize that it is time to stop counting how many go to college and ask instead how many succeed.

Promoting Success

The argument in this chapter is that college admission is no longer a legitimate goal for the nation or its schools. Open admissions and need-based, not merit-based, financial aid programs have removed barriers for most teens. Within 2 years after graduation, more than 70% of high school graduates have tried college. But more than half fail to graduate from college; of those who do, at least one in three will not get a college-level job. All this occurs at great expense to teens, their parents, and the nation. Thus, the new goal, the ethical goal, should be working to improve postsecondary success.

Ways students may improve their likelihood of postsecondary success is the subject of this book. The premise is that success for this generation of teens depends on both academic maturity and career maturity. Although much can still be done to improve academics, particularly for those in the academic middle, the focus of this book is to create an understanding of the concept of career maturity so that teens can be helped to make better reality-based choices that have a higher probability of success. One aspect of career maturity is a basic understanding of the labor market. At the heart of the "one way to win" mentality are many incorrect and/or inaccurate labor market perceptions that result in bad advice being given to teens. Thus, the three chapters in Part 1 deal with three aspects of the labor market. The discussion in Chapter 2 focuses on persistent myths and bad advice. Chapter 3 deals with the important bottom line: If "other ways to win" exist, what are they? Finally, Chapter 4 addresses the need to create opportunity by countering occupational stereotypes.

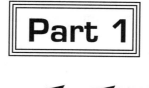

Part 1

Understanding Labor Market Fundamentals and Opportunities

As argued in Chapter 1, it's time to change the nation's focus from the number of students going to college to the number of students who succeed. For those high school graduates who go on to college, success is defined as (a) not being required to take remedial courses, (b) graduating on time, and then (c) finding employment commensurate with the level and type of education pursued. Furthermore, success depends as much on commitment as on academic skills. Commitment, in turn, requires a goal. Most teens prepare for their future careers right after high school, and their commitment comes from having realistic career direction.

Thus, it can be argued that promoting success in this generation depends on the acquisition of academics and the students' willingness to "get real" about themselves and the future they will face. Most teens indicate that finding a good job is among their top priorities, if not the most important priority, for their future, and "getting real" about themselves and the labor market they will face is of particular importance.

Many teens buy into the "one way to win" mentality because they think it is based on labor market realities. It would be more accurate to say that its basis rests on misinterpretations of labor market realities, as well as a large dose of misinformation and bad advice. One purpose of Part 1 is to address labor market misconceptions that lead many youths to make bad decisions and that lead well-meaning adults to give very bad advice. A second purpose is to provide detailed information about mostly undiscovered career opportunities. A third purpose is to address the harmful effects that occupational stereotyping plays in preventing youths from realizing their true potential.

Chapter 2

Labor Market Misunderstanding and Bad Advice

It may be stated with almost mathematical certainty that more than half of today's high school graduates will pursue postsecondary plans that result in failure. In a majority of cases, parents, teachers, guidance counselors, and just about everyone else support these plans; if they don't, they look the other way. Why? One reason is gross and general misunderstanding about future labor markets. The purpose of this chapter is threefold: (a) to clear up some widely held misconceptions about work, (b) to discuss how persons of all ages can successfully compete for high-skill/high-wage employment, and (c) to conduct a reality check on two pieces of bad advice given to teens about postponing career decisions until the college years.

One of the first things that those who seek to convince teens—and their parents—to "get real" need to realize is that labor market misunderstandings will work against their efforts. Correcting these misunderstandings must therefore be an early instructional objective of career development programs.

Following are discussions of three of the most widely held misconceptions leading to poor postsecondary planning among teens. Each either supports the "one way to win" misconception or acts to discourage youths from "getting real" about themselves and their future in the labor market.

21

Misunderstanding 1: High-Tech
Careers Require a University Degree

One reason why most youths opt to attend a university rather than consider alternatives is they believe that the best future opportunities will be in technical areas and that these occupations all will require a 4-year degree. During the 1990s, the press constantly reminded the public about declines in demand for unskilled labor and increases in demand for skilled labor and that technical areas were providing the fastest growth in high-skill/high-wage jobs. The public in general, and teens and their parents in particular, assumed that higher skills and technical work implied the need for a university education. This assumption simply is not true. In fact, most of this type of work will not require a 4-year or higher degree.

Although it is true that the ratio of unskilled to skilled work continues to decline, the skills in question are not necessarily of the type associated with higher education. In most occupations, the level of basic literacy skills has increased, as has the need to be a self-learner and problem solver. This hardly means, however, that everyone needs a university degree. U.S. Department of Labor projections actually paint a far different picture: Despite rising skills standards, 40% of all jobs and 43% of job openings will require only minimal on-the-job training through the year 2006 (Silvestri, 1997). Only 23% of jobs are projected to require preparation at the undergraduate or graduate level (see Table 2.1).

Nonetheless, it is true that, for this generation, many of the fastest growing occupations will be in technical areas and will require some postsecondary training. The word to be stressed, however, is *some*. Appropriate training for the majority of technical jobs is provided in pre-bachelor's degree postsecondary technical education, in the military, and by employers. For example, according to the American Electronics Association, high-tech industries—meaning those that manufacture computer-based hardware and software—now make up the largest manufacturing employer in the country, paying wages 73% higher than the average private-sector job, yet only 2% of Microsoft's entire workforce are 4-year college-educated computer programmers.

The bottom line is that only about one quarter of all technical work will require a university degree. Of the top 10 job titles identified by *Computer World*'s job forecast (December 29, 1997 issue) as

TABLE 2.1 Percentage of Employment Requiring Various Levels of Education and Training: 1996 & 2006

	1996	2006
First Professional	1.3%	1.3%
Doctorate	.8%	.8%
Master's	1.0%	1.0%
Bachelor's & experience	6.8%	7.0%
Bachelor's	12.0%	13.1%
Associate	3.1%	3.3%
Work experience in related occupation	6.1%	5.8%
Long-term on-the-job training	8.3%	7.9%
Moderate on-the-job training	12.7%	12.1%
Short-term on-the-job training	40.4%	40.2%

SOURCE: Data from Silvestri (1997).

being in the most demand, 6 could be performed by individuals trained on the job or at the pre-bachelor's degree level. Currently, only 25% of technical employment requires a university degree, and this percentage is not projected to change. What is happening, however, is that the share of the high-tech employment pie that requires some college is getting bigger. Importantly, in many of these areas, the supply of individuals with 1- or 2-year degrees is smaller than the demand for their services, whereas there is a worldwide over-supply of engineers.

Misunderstanding 2: A University Degree Guarantees Access to Professional Occupations and High Wages

Many teens opt to pursue university degrees because they think it will be a first-class ticket to professional or managerial jobs and thus high wages. It is difficult to be a regular consumer of the media without encountering in news accounts the fact that 4-year college graduates earn more than high school graduates. By 1993, for example, it was reported that university graduates earned 50% more than high school graduates. The lesson implied, whether overtly or covertly, is that those with 4-year degrees will make 50% more than those without them. The reasoning is seductively simple and thus appealing. The reasoning is appealing because in the past it was true: A university degree was a virtual guarantee of access to professional/managerial employment. Many parents who grew up in the 1960s found this to be the case. Unfortunately, for this generation, it is no longer true. Why? Because today there are more 4-year college graduates than there is commensurate employment.

Whereas in the past a 4-year degree was likened to an express ticket to professional or managerial employment, today it is more analogous to a ticket to an oversold airline flight, oversold because everyone has the same destination in mind. Of course, some will get on the plane; many, however, will not, instead joining the ranks of the underemployed. In the 1960s, only one in seven who earned a 4-year college degree failed to find college-level work. Today, it is, at best, one in three, and in the professions it is closer to one in two.

Higher education institutions frequently brag about how low unemployment rates are for college graduates. In 1998, for example, the rate for this group was reported to be 1.7%. Such figures are meaningless, however, because the issue is not how many university graduates are employed, but how many are holding jobs that require a 4-year degree. A 4-year college graduate working at the mall is technically unemployed. One wonders whether that person would count her- or himself as a college success story.

The National Center for Public Policy and Higher Education candidly points out that a college degree no longer guarantees (even) the probability of a good job and a place in the middle class. Instead, today, at best, it can only offer the hope of a place in line (Callan, 1998). As is discussed in the next section, the challenge for this generation is not just to get in line, but to get a seat on the plane. Most are holding the wrong ticket.

As argued in the book *Other Ways to Win* (Gray & Herr, 1995), the real tragedy is that those who are the most unlikely to graduate and the most likely to be holding the wrong ticket if they do are those from the academic middle. Importantly, new evidence suggests that even if they graduate, those who begin college with less than adequate academic skills and ability are the most likely also to end up underemployed. Pryor and Schaffer (1997) found that the best predictor of future earnings among university graduates was, in fact, their level of literacy when they graduated. Although some defy the odds and persist to graduate, students who enter college with poor academic skills graduate with relatively poor skills and end up in low-wage employment.

Misunderstanding 3: Career Planning Is Worthless Because People Change Jobs All the Time Anyway

Those who seek to improve the career maturity of today's youths will quickly encounter the belief that career planning is futile because the world of work is constantly changing, leading people to take a series and variety of jobs. Faced with this reality, many use this likelihood as a rationale for not making career decisions at all, preferring instead to take a wait-and-see attitude. This belief stems, in part, from confusing jobs with careers.

Jobs and careers are not the same things. Although for a few, a single job may also be their career, a *career* is typically defined as a series of related jobs over time. Importantly, although changing jobs is common, changing careers is not. One way to illustrate this point is to list all the jobs one has held and then to group them into careers. For most adults, the jobs list will be long and the career list short. Even though holding multiple jobs is expected and is a characteristic of a very successful wage earnings history, pursuing multiple careers is more often a sign of a troubled work history and below-average earnings. Equally important, career changes often involve moving to a related career, using the skills gained in one to pursue another. Thus, even among those who have had multiple careers, these careers are often closely related. When they are not, the individuals are probably good candidates for career counseling.

The goal of career maturity efforts is to help youths make tentative decisions regarding career interests, not to help them pick jobs. Teens will probably hold many jobs in their lifetimes, but few hope to pursue many careers. Graduating from high school with verified yet tentative career interests leads to both postsecondary success and a stable career pattern later in life. Teens have two choices: They can let fate and labor market Darwinism decide their future, or they can be proactive and plan for success. If success is defined as getting high-skill/high-wage work—and for most teens this is at least part of the definition—then a prerequisite is gaining an understanding of what they need to compete for good jobs. Is a degree enough? No, it is no longer enough.

Finding the Labor Market Advantage: The Secret to Getting High-Skill/ High-Wage Employment

The expressed goal of virtually all high school graduates is to find a career that will ensure them a solid place in the middle class. Career-mature persons know how to prepare for this goal. Specifically, they are aware of what leads to the labor market advantage needed to apply successfully for jobs that are both satisfying and financially rewarding. Thus, efforts to promote success by fostering career maturity need to address this issue.

Competition for High-Wage Employment

This generation's dilemma stems from the declining percentage of the types of work that will enable them to realize their hopes and dreams. In the past, for example, youths could always count on the fact that if all else failed, they could probably land jobs in a low- or semiskilled manufacturing area that paid good wages and benefits. This generation does not have this type of fallback: Low-skill/high-wage work has gone abroad, and the number of semiskilled/high-wage jobs in manufacturing continues to decline.

As illustrated in Table 2.1, the stark reality is that even in the year 2006, only about 26% of all work will require a postsecondary education; a persistent 40% of all employment will be in jobs that require little skill. As shown in Table 2.2, 43% of those university graduates will likely be underemployed by 2006. The implication is clear: The competition of a lifetime for this generation will focus on being one of the winners of high-skill/high-wage work. The question is, How? According to conventional "wisdom," college is the key.

As discussed previously, confronted with the reality of limited high-wage employment, most teens, their parents, and everyone else have concluded that the answer is higher education. Yet, as demonstrated in Table 2.2, college clearly will not be sufficient, nor guarantee success, for all who try. The demand for those earning a bache-

TABLE 2.2 Comparison of Occupation Supply and Demand by Higher Education Credential to the Year 2006

	Supply	*Demand*	*% Underemployed*
First Professional	79,300	58,200	27%
Doctorate	47,900	46,000	3%
Master's	450,000	43,000	90%
Bachelor's	1,268,000	734,300	43%

SOURCE: "Projections of Educational Statistics to 2007" (1997).

lor's degree, for example, will be only 57% of the number credentialed in 2006; thus, 43% face underemployment, which is close to one in two. The outlook for those who would avoid underemployment by going back for a master's degree is the worst: Employment opportunities may be available for only 1 in 10. Importantly, these supply figures do not take into account individuals with similar credentials from past years who are still looking, nor recent immigrants to the United States; thus, if anything, the data underestimate the supply side and underemployment figures.

To summarize the situation, let's return to the comparison of a college graduate with a person who has a ticket for an oversold flight. Clearly, more people have tickets than seats. What can an individual do to gain an advantage for getting on the plane? Having a degree is not enough; everyone has one. Somehow the person needs to look different from the others in line. Such an advantage in the workforce is called *labor market advantage*. One way to get a clue to the sources of labor market advantage is to read the Sunday newspaper.

The Sunday Morning Research Project

The situation for this generation can be summarized as too many teens for too few high-skill/high-wage jobs. Having a degree only guarantees a place in line. How does one get through the door and get hired?

Three theories are often presented regarding the credentials sought by employers. The first theory is most often heard from employers who desire potential employees with good work ethics: *Necessary training will be provided on the job.* The second theory—one that is particularly attractive to liberal arts college faculty—is that *employers are looking for individuals with good academic skills who have learned to think; employers will provide the training.* The third theory is the old-fashioned idea that *employers will always prefer candidates with prior relevant work skills.* To discover which of the three theories is correct, pick up a copy of a metro area Sunday newspaper and check the Help Wanted section. Do ads state that the only qualifications are "come to work on time and be cooperative" or even the ability to read, write, and do algebra? No! One finds instead job titles most of us do not understand and lists of minimum qualifications that suggest employers are looking for people who can do very specific things.

As illustrated in Figure 2.1, labor market advantage comes from three types of entry-level skills. Positive work ethics, such as initiative and cooperation, are the prerequisite for all employment. Everyone knows someone with many degrees and no job because the person does not have the interpersonal skills to hold a job. Furthermore, for some types of employment—namely, low-skill/low-wage employment—work ethics are all that is needed. Thus, an employer who indicates that all she or he needs is teens with good work ethics is probably hiring low-wage workers.

As work becomes more skilled, academic skills become important. In fact, when labor experts talk of work becoming more skilled, they are noting the level of basic literacy skills required. Employers' preference for college graduates for non-college-level jobs stems from the belief that a degree means good academic skills. If, however, the goal is high-skill/high-wage employment, the advantage goes to those with specific occupational skills. A National Federation of Independent Businesses poll found, for example, that occupational/job skill was the ability most sought; next to last in demand were reading, writing, and mathematics reasoning abilities (Bishop, 1995).

Does this mean that academic skills are unimportant? No, but their relative importance is overstated. The only academic skill

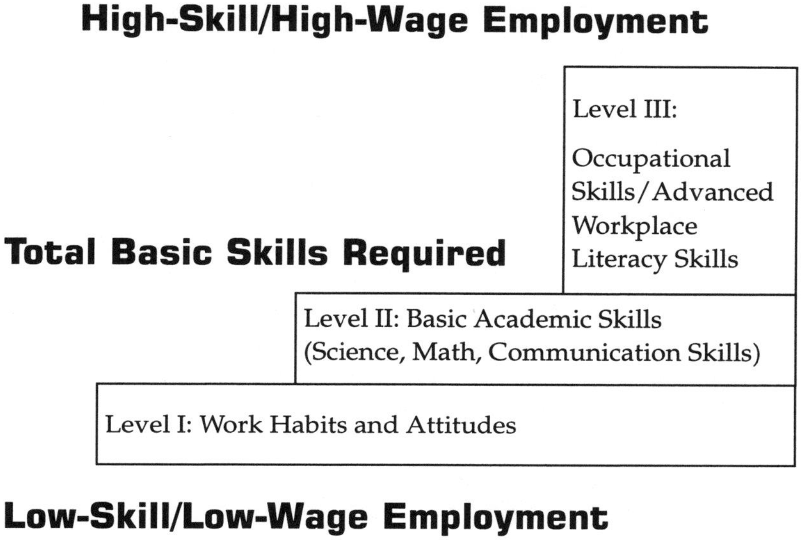

High-Skill/High-Wage Employment

Total Basic Skills Required

	Level III: Occupational Skills/Advanced Workplace Literacy Skills

Level II: Basic Academic Skills (Science, Math, Communication Skills)

Level I: Work Habits and Attitudes

Low-Skill/Low-Wage Employment

Figure 2.1. Sources of labor market advantage.

found to be highly correlated with worker productivity is math reasoning ability (Bishop, 1995); the best predictor is technical skills. Importantly, academic skills are a good predictor of success in training. In reality, though, and despite rhetoric to the contrary, most workers use very few academic skills on the job (Pucel, 1995). What counts are technical skills. Those in line with technical skills or experience that demonstrates technical skills get on the plane first.

Raising the Skills Bar

The late 1990s saw significant press coverage about the shortage of college graduates. A closer look at the details, however, suggested that the shortage was not of college graduates but of graduates with skills, particularly computer-related information technology skills. The skill set required for these occupations has become very specific. These are not skills that can be taught quickly on the job. Nor can firms in the highly competitive computer environment afford to wait for employees to be trained sufficiently. Thus, only those with the skills are hired.

The effect of this development is analogous to raising the skills bar or threshold at the hiring door. Those who cannot step over the threshold are not considered. For example, in 1996 the press reported a dramatic shortage of professionals in a very high-paying occupation—computer animation programmers. For every person being trained, three jobs were open. Importantly, the vast majority of those with computer animation skills did not graduate from universities but from 1- and 2-year art schools and institutes. Having a degree did not qualify applicants; they needed very specific programming skills. The raising of the skills bar has, in fact, lessened the importance of academic degrees and increased the importance of industry "certificates" directly related to skills, such as knowledge of the computer language NOVEL. The message is clear:

> For this generation, demonstrated skills, not degrees, count in competing for high-wage employment.

The implication of Figure 2.1 for today's youths is obvious: The way to look unique in line is to have the specific skill set desired by those employing high-skill/high-wage workers. There are two reasons for this reality. First, as already mentioned, there are now more people in line for most, though not all (see Chapter 3), high-wage employment than there are opportunities; thus, employers can afford to be choosy. It used to be that the way to look different—to gain advantage over others in line—was to carry a degree and good grades. This is no longer the case: Today, there are more people in line with good grades than there are opportunities. Employers are looking for evidence that individuals can apply what they know in their core industry. Thus, co-op experiences, summer employment, and internships are as important as grades because they demonstrate skill and commitment.

Perhaps the most telling evidence of the dominance of skills over degrees in competing for high-wage employment is the growing ranks of "reverse transfers." In a national study of students enrolled in information technology career preparation programs, 80% were found to have some previous college experience. Although some percentage of this group are incumbent workers seeking to upgrade their skills, many also are college graduates stuck in low-skill/low-wage employment (http://www.aiminstitute.org/studies/nonrad/p02.htm).

Will University Graduates Take All the Good Jobs?

A 4-year college degree may get a person a place in line for high-wage employment, but that is all it gets. Too many people are in line. In some occupations, particularly those related to computer applications, the low number in line is attributable to the very specific nature of the skills required for most positions and the fact that few people have those skills.

The obvious implication of the oversupply of college graduates will not be missed by teens or parents. It does not take a labor market expert to conclude that college graduates who cannot find college-level work will start taking jobs that used to go to high school graduates or those with lower degrees. One only has to visit the local mall to realize that this belief contains some truth. More analytical data are presented in Table 2.3. Clearly, since the 1970s, the percentage of both 4-year college graduates and those who attended but did not graduate who are employed in high-school-level jobs has increased substantially. In the case of university graduates, it has almost doubled.

Does this mean that the only hope is to get a university degree even if it only means obtaining a high-school-level job? No! The important point is that even though college graduates are displacing those without degrees, this is occurring primarily in low-skill/low-wage employment. University graduates are not displacing individuals with specific occupational skills. Remember the case mentioned earlier regarding computer animation programmers. Individuals with these skills have no need to worry about being displaced by art majors from universities.

At the same time, it is clear that individuals who fail to develop postsecondary plans that lead to occupational skills, be they in higher education, the military, an apprentice program, or formal on-the-job training, will be at a disadvantage. In low-wage/low-skill employment, then, those with degrees will probably displace those

TABLE 2.3 Percentage of College-Educated Workers in High School Jobs: 1971 and 1995

	1971	1995
Some University Courses	13%	20%
University Degree	17%	30%

SOURCE: Data from Pryor and Schaffer (1997).

with few marketable skills. But they will not displace those with specific occupational skills in demand.

Of course, some university degrees result in marketable skills, whereas others do not. Some result in marketable skills but too many people graduate each year with those skills. Even among those with good grades, the line is still too long; those with relevant co-op, internship, or summer work experience will probably end up employed. Thus, picking the correct program to pursue in college or elsewhere is crucial. Unfortunately, advising teens to wait until college to sort this out is terrible advice.

Bad Advice Given to Teens

Chapter 1 reported evidence that suggests the majority of today's youths graduate from high school and pursue plans that lead, with mathematical certainty, to failure. Most, in fact, graduate with no plans, which is a large part of the problem. Yet, as also has been pointed out, it is not necessarily the teens' fault. Generally, both educators and parents have been ambivalent about career planning for high school students. The values that underlie this uncertainty are manifested in two widely held conventional points of wisdom. The first is the belief that making career decisions reduces opportunity by somehow "closing doors" to future opportunity. The second pertains to the lack of career-related focus by high school seniors: This is "not a cause for concern because they will surely decide later in college." Before ending this chapter, let's look at these two conventional points of "wisdom." These points may have been sound in past generations, but for this generation, they are just plain bad advice.

Closing Doors and Deciding on College: A Personal Anecdote

During my senior year in high school, I was a rather frequent visitor to the guidance counselor. I was applying to colleges: I needed help! Although, admittedly, this was some time ago, one visit has always stuck in my mind. My counselor asked me what my career interests were. I was speechless; I had no answer. In fact, I was surprised to be asked. After all, I was going to college, not to work.

I recall being tempted to say "ceramics engineering." I remembered someone saying this was going to be a great field. As it turned out, the person was right, but with an SAT math score that still had quite a ways to go to reach 600, even I knew this was fantasy. I did not know much else. In fact, I was clueless about my career interests. Clinically, I was a classic example of career immaturity.

At any rate, I decided to play it straight and simply say that I had not yet decided. To my surprise, my counselor was neither surprised nor concerned. Instead of a lecture on the need to get focused, she assured me that my uncertainty was not unusual and "not to worry" because I would discover my career interests in college. In fact, she warned me about making career decisions too early; after all, I did not want to "close any doors."

Unfortunately, despite her predictions, I graduated 4 years later still uncertain about what I was now going to do. Four years of a liberal arts education in the middle of Maine had not resulted in any great revelations regarding my life's calling. Fortunately for me, my uncertainty did not matter much anyway. The war in Vietnam was in full swing, and the economy was booming. If you were breathing and had a college degree, you were in the driver's seat. After a brief stint in advertising sales, I ended up being a high school teacher. The school system actually called me. School was opening in 3 days. I had a BA in economics, but I ended up teaching English. That was 30 years ago. The labor market my generation faced was unlike the one to be encountered by this generation. The harsh reality for this generation is that all doors to high-skill/high-wage employment are closed.

The belief that making career decisions somehow limits opportunities and thus should be avoided as long as possible is part of the American mystique. The argument in this book is that the opposite is now true. For most teens, postponing career decisions is a good indication of probable postsecondary failure. Importantly, the fact that many never decide in all likelihood means a lifelong troubled work history in low-skill/low-wage employment. These individuals literally never get on track.

The fallacy of the warning about closing doors resides in the assumption implied in the comment itself. At its root is the implication that the doors to all careers are open. If this were the case, career decisions could be postponed indefinitely; when the time came, a person could choose a career and be assured of success. Clearly, this was never the case, but in today's labor market, this is completely false. The only occupational doors that are open lead to low-skill/low-wage work. The doors that lead to high-skill/high-wage employment are all closed because either more individuals are in line than there are jobs, or the skills needed to get a job offer are so specific that applicants without these skills are not considered. Thus, it is argued that:

This generation does not have to worry about closing doors to high-skill/high-wage work: they are already closed. The number one concern is how to open doors.

As discussed previously in this chapter, for this generation, the key to opening the door to high-skill/high-wage employment is having the relevant skills—not just generic academic skills or good grades, but evidence that one can perform on the job in very specific ways. This objective should be among the most important in formulating postsecondary plans. But a prerequisite decision is implied.

Choosing a Door to Open

If the route to labor market advantage in competing for high-skill/high-wage employment is not degrees but occupational skills or experience, then developing these skills becomes the first step. The problem is that the skill sets are different for different occupations. Despite what liberal arts educators may preach, one cannot realistically try to develop skills that will open many different occupational doors. Thus, deciding which door or related doors to open becomes the prerequisite to postsecondary success.

> For this generation, opening doors to high-skill/high-wage employment requires first deciding which door to attempt to pass through and how to acquire the necessary skills.

"Choosing a door to open" is a useful way to think about making career decisions. The ability to make an informed choice signals efforts toward career maturity. Choosing a single door to open, especially for high school students, is not necessary or even desirable. High school graduates, however, should have narrowed choices to several (and, one hopes, related) doors. The important point to remember is the goal to open a door; the sooner a decision is made about which doors to line up for, the sooner skills can be acquired as needed to move toward desirable employment. Of course, some people will still suggest that this is best done in college.

Postponing Career Decisions Until College

It is interesting to note that, often, those who counsel high school students against making tentative career decisions too early for fear of closing doors also believe that the right time is just a few years or even months later when the teens are in college. Those who hold this belief should think back to their college years to test the wisdom of this advice. The reality is that universities and colleges are both very expensive and not very good places to be making career decisions.

Postponing career decisions until the college years is a very bad idea. Why? First, many students never last more than a year; one reason they leave is their lack of career maturity. Second, effective career planning requires the opportunity to verify choices in the real world; in fact, however, fewer places are more detached from reality than colleges and universities. Third, the adults most often encountered by college students—namely, the faculty—are less than disinterested parties; most know that their jobs depend on students choosing their disciplines as majors.

The best evidence that postponing career decisions until college is a very bad idea, however, comes from looking at the number of college students who drop out when they have to chose a major. There seems to be a faith or hope that, at some point in the students' early college years, they will experience an epiphany that will lead to a clear career focus. Other than hoping that their child will graduate, the desire for this revelation is probably the primary prayer of tuition-paying parents. Unfortunately, with few exceptions, it just does not happen. As argued earlier, reality can be postponed, but few can avoid it. It is much better and cheaper to face reality—to "get real"—in the high school years.

Promoting Success

Improving the incidence of postsecondary success among today's teens requires efforts to increase their general level of career maturity and direction, which in turn requires efforts to correct misconceptions shared by them, as well as by their parents and teachers. Labor market misconceptions are one major factor in the widespread belief in the "one way to win" mentality. Opening a door to high-wage employment is a source of lifelong competition for this generation. Today's youths do not have to worry about closing doors; the only doors open are those that lead to low-skill/low-wage work. The secret to opening doors to high-skill/high-wage employment is skills, and skills can be developed only when teens are able to decide which doors (careers) they will attempt to pass through. Choosing a career, however, requires knowing about various opportunities behind the doors. On the basis of national surveys, today's youths seem to have concluded that only one set of doors holds any potential at all—namely, the set that leads to professional careers. But there are other ways to win in the labor market. This is the topic of Chapter 3.

Other Ways to Win

Alternative Career Opportunities

For some teens, graduation from high school means a transition from school to work; for most, it means more schooling. Sooner or later, however, virtually all must deal with the big "W"—namely, work. Prospects for an attractive career rank first among reasons for matriculating as reported by teens. Although there may be many routes to take after high school—the topic of Chapter 7—in the end the destination is a career. Logic suggests, therefore, that high school students should graduate with some level of specificity for a career or group of careers. As argued previously, those who do not do so either fail to graduate or do not find commensurate employment if they do.

The purpose of this chapter is to provide an overview of career opportunities through the year 2006 based on U.S. Department of Labor projections. These data are provided as background information for professionals developing instruction that promotes teen career maturity. Perhaps uniquely, the emphasis is not on careers requiring a university education or graduate school, but on high-skill/high-wage nonprofessional careers that typically a person prepares for in pre-bachelor's degree postsecondary technical education, apprenticeship programs, the military, and so on. These careers are the best-kept secrets in America and provide the best opportunity and the best return on investment of tuition dollars, particularly for high schoolers who graduate from the academic middle of their senior class.

This chapter has two sections. The first section presents U.S. Department of Labor projections for the fastest growing occupations, presents some cautions about the use of this type of information, and looks at one industry—information technology—as an example. The second section explores a variety of high-skill/high-wage occupations that do not require a university degree and provides sources of additional information.

Using Labor Market Information

Information on opportunities in the labor market is abundant. The topic appears to be a favorite of the press, and the public is always interested. Although the sources of such information are usually U.S. Department of Labor reports and projections, industry groups, particularly when faced with labor shortages, also will disseminate data. All too often, what is reported or the way it is interpreted leads to the wrong conclusions by the public. Thus, helping teens develop career maturity includes helping them become more savvy consumers of labor market information. The first thing to remember is that, from the perspective of a person trying to enter the labor market, knowing the extent of the competition (supply) is as important as knowing the number of projected job openings (demand).

Supply: The Forgotten Variable

With few exceptions, the labor market information provided in the mass media is limited to job opening or demand-side data. Effective planning requires both demand-side and supply-side data because effective postsecondary planning based on a career focus includes a consideration of the extent of future opportunities. Such analysis requires having estimates for job openings and numbers of job applicants. The situation is analogous to a couple deciding on Friday that they want to get away for a weekend to the shore or to do a little skiing. Of course, they lack lodging reservations. No problem. Tourist information indicates that 10,000 hotel rooms are available where they want to go. That may be, but what if 20,000 like-

TABLE 3.1 Occupational Groups Ranked by Earnings, Net
Opportunities, and Total Employment (numbers in
thousands: projections through 2006)

Occupational Group	Earnings Rank	Net Opportunities Rank	Total Jobs 2006
Managerial/ Professional	1	6	38,864
Craft/Precision Manufacturing/ Specialized Repair	2	3	15,448
Technical Support (includes Clerical)	3	1	29,706
Service	4	4	25,147
Operative/Laborer	5	2	19,365
Farming/Fishing	6	5	3,823

minded individuals also want to get away for the weekend and are
headed to the same destination? Suddenly, the number 10,000 does
not seem quite so large. Such is the case with labor market numbers
indicating thousands of openings; such figures are meaningless because often tens of thousands are competing for these opportunities.
Table 3.1 illustrates this point.

The first column in Table 3.1 lists the six major occupational
groups within the economy; all occupations are included in one of
these six categories. The second column ranks the occupational
groups by earnings. The third column ranks the groups by net job
opportunities, meaning the number of job seekers is subtracted from
the number of annual openings. Note that Managerial/Professional
is ranked first in terms of earnings, which is probably why at least
half of all teens indicate a vague preference for this type of employment. But also note that, in terms of net opportunity, Managerial/
Professional is ranked last despite the fact that, in terms of total employment, it is also the largest group. The reason is simple: There are

about twice as many college graduates with degrees in these fields annually than there are jobs, and this does not take immigration into consideration. Meanwhile, the second smallest group in terms of total employment—Craft/Precision Manufacturing/Specialized Repair—is ranked second in terms of earnings and third in terms of opportunity, making it, in general, a far more attractive option. This does not necessarily mean that some teens should not aspire to Managerial/Professional occupations; after all, one in every two will be able to pursue a career in the highest paying occupational group. But it does mean that the competition will be fierce; for those from the academic middle who enter college the least academically prepared and therefore attend the least prestigious colleges, it is a long shot.

Fastest Growing Versus Greatest Opportunity

One of the most popular and thus most often publicized type of labor market forecast is the list of the fastest growing occupations. The assumption is that *fastest growing* means "greatest opportunity." Wrong! Table 3.2 lists the top 20 fastest growing occupations; Table 3.3 lists occupations projected to add the largest number of additional jobs. Notice that few occupations are on both lists. Also, neither is a good indicator of total jobs. For example, whereas predictions are that the occupations Systems Analyst and Cashier will add about the same total number of jobs (see Table 3.3), there will be about three Cashier jobs for every Systems Analyst job.

"Fastest growing" and "greatest job growth" have nothing to do with total opportunity. For example, the fastest growing occupational group, Database Administrator/Computer Scientist, is predicted to add 249,000 jobs, but even with this growth, total employment will be only 0.003% of the total labor force. The reality is that "fastest growing" is much more a function of the low number of jobs in the base year than anything else.

Another lesson to be learned from these data is evident after examining the numbers for earnings quartile and typical training required for these occupations. "Fastest growing" and "greatest job growth" also have nothing to do with earnings. Of the 20 fastest growing jobs (Table 3.2), 7 are in the two lowest paying quartiles; of the 20 greatest in growth (Table 3.3), 10 are in the two lowest paying quartiles. Also notice that the numbers of jobs in these low-paying/

TABLE 3.2 Fastest Growing Occupations, 1996-2006 (numbers in thousands)

Occupation	Job Growth 1996-2006	Income Quartile Rank	Education/ Training Required
Database Administrator/ Computer Scientist	249	1	BS
Computer Engineer	235	1	BS
Systems Analyst	520	1	BS
Home Care Aide	171	4	OJT
Physical Therapy Aide	66	4	OJT
Home Health Aide	378	4	OJT
Medical Assistant	166	3	OJT
Desktop Publisher	22	2	ASS
Physical Therapist	81	1	BS
Occupational Therapist Aide	11	3	ASS
Paralegal	76	2	ASS
Occupational Therapist	38	1	BS
Special Education Teacher	241	1	BS
Human Services Worker	98	4	OJT
Computer Repairer	42	2	ASS
Medical Records Technician	44	2	ASS
Speech Therapist	44	1	MS
Dental Hygienist	64	1	ASS
Recreation Attendant	138	3	OJT
Physician's Assistant	30	1	BS

SOURCE: Data from Silvestri (1997).

NOTE: ASS = associate degree; BS = bachelor of science degree; MS = master of science degree; OJT = on-the-job training.

TABLE 3.3 Occupations With Greatest Job Growth, 1996-2006 (numbers in thousands)

Occupation	Job Growth 1996-2006	Income Quartile Rank	Education/ Training Required
Cashier	530	4	OJT
Systems Analyst	520	1	BS
Manager	467	1	BS
Registered Nurse	411	1	ASS
Retail Salesperson	488	3	OJT
Truck Driver	404	2	OJT/Cert.
Home Health Aide	378	4	OJT/Cert.
Teacher's Aide	370	4	OJT/Cert.
Nurse's Aide	333	4	Cert.
Receptionist/Clerk	318	4	OJT
High School Teacher	312	1	BS
Child Care Worker	299	4	OJT/Cert.
Office Manager	262	2	ASS
Database Manager	249	1	BS
Retail Supervisor	246	2	BS/ASS
Maintenance Worker	246	4	OJT
Fast-Foods Worker	243	4	OJT
Special Education Teacher	241	1	BS
Computer Engineer	235	1	BS
Food Service Worker	234	4	OJT

SOURCE: Data from Silvestri (1997).

NOTE: ASS = associate degree; BS = bachelor of science degree; Cert. = certificate; OJT = on-the-job training.

fast-growing occupations far exceed the numbers in the high-paying/fast-growing areas.

A Case Study: Information Technology Workers

It seems that, rather routinely, certain occupations become "hot," at least in the eyes of the news media and thus the public. Thinking back, one remembers, for example, when oceanography and marine biology were the rage, then came robotics, and then fiber optics. Higher education institutions started new programs, and students enrolled. But the predicted boom in marine biology never materialized; automated manufacturing did not create a huge demand for a new type of technician; and fiber optics was, in fact, just another new material that is now installed by electricians. These illustrations suggest caution in predictions based on hot occupations. This includes information technology (IT), the "darling" occupation of the late 1990s.

According to the Information Technology Association of America (ITA, 1998), 190,000 jobs went unfilled in 1998; this claim is supported by U.S. Department of Labor projections of 1.3 million new IT jobs through 2006. Of importance to this discussion, the focus of these efforts was entirely on the need for individuals trained at the university level. A study conducted for ITA and widely disseminated by the association, for example, looked at only three types of IT workers—programmers, systems analysts, and computer engineers—and reported that a bachelor's degree is required for all or most of the positions. The message would seem to be this: Get a 4-year degree in computer science. Closer examination by the General Accounting Office (GAO) suggested a different message, however.

Asked by Congress to assess the alleged shortage of IT workers, the GAO examined the ITA study and concluded that it had counted only those trained at the university level, thus dramatically overestimating the shortage. Work by the National Science Foundation (NSF) found, for example, that only 25% of current programmers have degrees in computer science. Some individuals saw a more sinister motive afoot, suggesting that ITA's real motive was to ensure a steady, and thus cheap, supply of young computer science workers; as evidence, these individuals noted that the unemployment rate for programmers aged 50 and over was 17% and that only 19% of computer science majors were still in the field 20 years later. It was further revealed that the ITA study was based on a response rate of only 271 companies, or 14% of all those polled. Still others suggested that much of the current shortage was attributable to the need to reprogram computers for the year 2000 (Y2K) dilemma (Joyner, 1998).

Will IT provide significant opportunities in the future? Yes. Will most jobs go to university graduates? No. Like all technical employment, about 25% will require a university education; the rest will not. Some estimate that 85% of IT positions will be filled by current employees and other positions by temporary employees hired to do specific jobs; currently, 14% of all temporary workers are employed in IT occupations. The reality is that IT jobs cover a wide range of occupations, most of which can be trained for at the pre-bachelor's degree level. The point is that caution is needed when drawing conclusions based on information in the press or put out by trade associations. All too often, the implied message is "Get a university degree," when, in fact, most people whom information technology employers hire do not need one.

Guides for Using Labor Market Information

In the light of the all too frequent misinterpretation of labor market information, what guidelines can be given in using labor market information? The following eight guidelines are suggested.

1. To assess true opportunity, it is necessary to consider both the occupation outlook and the numbers of individuals credentialed for any particular occupation.

2. Do not confuse fastest growing or greatest job growth with real opportunity. Often, some of the slowest growing occupations provide the best opportunities.

3. The key to labor market advantage is developing demonstrable skill related to career goals, either because job openings are too few or because the skill set required to do the work is very specific.

4. Technical skills are the common characteristic of most occupations predicted to be in high demand.

5. The oversupply of university graduates will continue, when compared to the number of jobs requiring a university degree. Predictions are that 43% of all 4-year college graduates will go underemployed; only 23% of all employment will require a bachelor of arts degree.

6. The highest paying occupations will continue to be in the Managerial/Professional area, but competition will be fierce. At least one in two with the prerequisite credentials will be unsuccessful.

7. The second and third highest paying occupational groups are Craft/Precision Manufacturing/Specialized Repair and Technical Support. In most cases, a university degree is not required, and in many cases, demand for workers exceeds supply.

8. Thus, U.S. Department of Labor studies suggest that individuals who are successful in pursuing careers in occupations included in Craft/Precision Manufacturing/Specialized Repair will out-earn all university graduates except those who are successful in pursuing careers in the Managerial/Professional occupations.

Opportunities Without a Bachelor's Degree

The case has been made that there are "ways to win" other than a university degree. The point is not that some youths should seek careers requiring a university education, but that for many the propensity for success would be dramatically increased if they considered alternatives, especially those in the second and third highest paying occupational groups: Craft/Precision Manufacturing/Specialized Repair and Technical Support. This section lists specific examples. For those who would promote career maturity and other ways to win, having such a list of high-skill/high-wage nonprofessional occupations is of great help when working with teens and parents.

High-Skill/High-Wage
Nonprofessional Occupations

While the press promotes information technology (IT) and college, real opportunity for many teens is, in fact, elsewhere. The best opportunities, particularly for teens from the academic middle, are occupations that are high-skill and thus high-wage but do not require a university degree. These occupations are found in all industry groups, although they tend to be the most common in the Technical Support and Craft/Precision Manufacturing/Specialized Repair areas. The demand for these services is acute. For example, by the late 1990s, a housing shortage developed largely because of a shortage of skilled construction workers to build them. Thus, electricians, pipe fitters/plumbers, and masons were reported to be earning as much as $40 an hour.

Table 3.4 is a list of some of these occupations by major industrial category. All pay wages in the top two earning quartiles, and most require some formal training—pre-bachelor's degree postsecondary technical education, formal on-the-job training, apprenticeship programs, or the military.

Promoting Success

For most teens and their parents, a bright future includes high-skill/high-wage work. With this in mind, the number who do not think about how to make this happen is somewhat surprising. One reason, of course, is the widely held misconception about the labor market, a misconception that actually discourages career planning and encourages a whole rash of bad decisions. The purpose of Chapters 2 and 3 was to discuss these misconceptions and, by so doing, to provide a labor market rationale for efforts to foster greater career maturity among teens. Because the emphasis has always been on professional occupations, details were provided instead on opportunities in high-skill/high-wage employment that requires postsecondary education but at the pre-bachelor's degree level. Selecting a tentative career or a set of related careers as a focus in effective postsecondary planning is the end product of efforts to help teens "get real." As stated previously, however, youths cannot make such decisions when they do not have the necessary information. Teens are too often forced into a narrow range of choices by occupational stereotypes about what is appropriate for their gender, race, ethnicity, or sociocultural background. These issues are addressed in Chapter 4.

TABLE 3.4 High-Skill/High-Wage Nonprofessional
Occupations

I.   Information Technology
    Computer Network Administrator
    Web Page Creator/Administrator
    Computer Systems Installer and Maintenance Worker
    Computer Repair Technician
    Computer Applications Specialist
    Information Technical Consultant
    Data Retrieval Specialist
    Computer Training Specialist
    Communications Systems Installer and Repairer
    Communications Systems Technical Consultant
    Data Entry Worker/Processor
    Help Desk Worker
    Internet Designer, Developer, Administrator
    Technical Documentation Worker

II. Traditional Crafts
    Automotive Technician
    Precision Welder
    Pipe Fitter/Plumber
    Heating/Ventilation/Air Conditioning/Stationary Engineer
    Mason
    Customize Installer

III. Industrial Manufacturing Technology
    Computer Numeric Control Machine Tool Operator:
        Metal and Wood
    Tool and Die Maker
    Automated Manufacturing System Technician
    Computer-Aided Designer
    Millwright/Industrial Maintenance Worker
    Industrial Electrician

IV. Allied Health Careers
    Licensed Practical Nurse
    Dental Hygienist
    Surgical Technician

(continued)

TABLE 3.4 Continued

      Paramedic
      Radiologist
      Health Facilities Manager
      Dietary Manager
      Health Information Technician
      Cardiology Technologist
      Respiratory Therapist

  V. Service Industries
      Paralegal
      Professional Chef
      Recreation/Restaurant Manager
      Law Enforcement Worker
      Fire Fighter
      Court/Conference Reporter
      Interpreter
      Landscape Manager

  VI. Electronics
      Avionics
      Electronics Technician
      Electromechanical Repair Technician
      Mobile Electronics Installer and Repairer
      Medical/Surgical Electronics Repairer

VII. The Arts
      Animated Computer Designer
      Computer Graphics Designer
      Lighting Designer/Installer/Repairer
      Set Designer/Construction Worker
      Cinematographer
      Actor
      Custom Designer

Chapter 4

Creating Opportunities by Countering Stereotypes

When the goal is postsecondary success, not college admissions, career direction becomes as pivotal as academic skills. But teens cannot maximize their human potential if their career aspirations are limited by stereotypes. This is especially true when decisions are slanted by stereotypes regarding what is appropriate or possible on the basis of a teen's gender, race, ethnicity, socioeconomic (SES) status, or area of residence. Thus, helping teens "get real" often must include helping them move beyond these stereotypes. Similarly, those who would lead such efforts need to reflect on their own stereotypes to eliminate them. Although having such biases is natural, the challenge is to recognize and get over them.

Occupational Stereotypes

Arguably, each occupation/career has certain social connotations regarding its status and appropriateness. Both qualities are matters of concern because both serve to limit the range of careers teens will even consider. For example, teens are deeply infatuated with professional careers, an infatuation attributable, in large part, to the high social status enjoyed by such occupations. The problem is that only 20% of all work is professional; thus, the odds of landing such a job is fair to poor, but this obsession often makes teens unwilling to consider alternatives.

Although the status that society assigns to various careers tends to distort teens' career decision making, other types of stereotypes have a greater effect on women, people of color, those from impoverished homes, and those from geographically isolated regions. Take, for example, the stereotype that "all" teens of Asian descent are gifted students and thus should prepare for careers in the scholarly professions, whereas "all" teens of African American and Hispanic descent are relatively poor students and should enroll in junior colleges or go directly to work. Other misconceptions are that technical work is appropriate for men but not women and that being an elementary schoolteacher is appropriate for women but not men.

Stereotypes such as these are the focus of this chapter. Such stereotypes are powerful deterrents to teens making decisions that have a high probability for success. They may be even more powerful influences on the real gatekeepers—namely, parents. It is no coincidence that those few women who are willing to prepare for nontraditional careers typically indicate strong support from their parents. Such stereotypes often serve to discourage teens and sap their hope for the future. To deny the existence of such stereotypes is counterproductive. The best approach is to confront them openly, to teach teens to question the validity of such stereotypes for them, and to support teens when they have the courage to take the road less traveled.

Stereotypes Narrow Choices

Career decisions based on stereotypes limit opportunity. When youths either fail to consider or dismiss alternatives because of stereotypical views, they are narrowing their alternatives. In this case, the "old saw" about closing doors is true. Career decisions based on stereotypes do close doors. This point is illustrated in Table 4.1. The six major occupational groups, ranked by earnings, are presented here first, followed by the percentage of the workforce in each group that are women, African Americans, and Hispanics. Lacking biases and equal opportunity, the distribution could be similar to the percentage of the total labor force who are women (46.2%), African Americans (10.8%), and Hispanics (9.8%). Obviously, this is not the case. The percentage of the Managerial/Professional workforce that are women is about right, but they are severely underrepresented in the second highest paying occupational group (Craft/Precision

TABLE 4.1 Percentage of Occupational Groups Composed of
Women, African Americans, and Hispanics

Occupation (Ranked by Earnings)	Women	African Americans	Hispanics
Managerial/Professional	49%	7%	5%
Craft/Precision Manufacturing/ Specialized Repair	9%	8%	12%
Technical Support (includes Clerical)	64%	10%	8%
Service	60%	16%	15%
Operators/Laborers	25%	7%	15%
Farming	19%	1%	20%

SOURCE: U.S. Department of Labor (1998b).

Manufacturing/Specialized Repair) and overrepresented in the Technical (that includes Clerical occupations) and Service groups. African Americans are underrepresented in both of the two highest paying occupational groups but overrepresented in Service. Similar discrepancies can be noted for Hispanics. The distribution of teens from low-income homes, regardless of race, shows similar patterns: They are especially underrepresented in Managerial/Professional and overrepresented in Service and Operators/Laborers.

The reasons for the unequal distributions illustrated in Table 4.1 are many, varied, and complex and include discrimination and unequal access to postsecondary education. In the case of women, however, the reasons can also be stereotypical views regarding women and work.

Gender Stereotypes

Although all youths can benefit from opportunities to identify and verify career interests, teenage girls present a special case. More than 30 years ago, Congress passed the Equal Pay Act, which requires that women be paid the same wages as men for work done under similar conditions and requiring similar skills. Although progress has been made since, the gender wage gap persisted throughout the 1990s, at around 75 cents. Women are twice as likely to be at high risk of underemployment and eight times as likely to be at medium risk of underemployment as men (Mohamed, 1998). The reasons are important evidence of the need to provide career development activities for young girls that include the instructional objective of countering gender stereotypes.

In the 1960s, when the gender wage gap was about 60 cents, the most common explanation was that women were less likely to go to college and thus, having less human capital investment, earned less in the labor force. Yet, this argument is not persuasive today.

In 1994, 76% of girls attended postsecondary education within 2 years after high school graduation, compared with 69% of males, and the differences were the greatest at 4-year colleges. But even though a university degree has a positive effect on the earnings for both genders, the return for males is higher than for females. In other words, the financial payoff from getting a college degree is more for men than for women. Why? Because women tend to choose a limited number of career options even if they go to college. Researchers are now beginning to conclude that the remaining obstacle to wage parity is not educational inequality but inequality in the distribution of women among all occupational sectors (Gray & Huang, 1991).

Table 4.2 indicates the degree to which a variety of variables affect the yearly income of young men versus young women. The higher the number (parameter estimate), the greater the effect of this variable on income. For example, completing the college prep program in high school has a positive effect on future earnings; this effect is almost twice as powerful for men as for women. Meanwhile, living in a rural area has a negative effect on future earnings but, again, more so for females than for males. Notice that the parameter estimates for college graduate and graduate school are also higher for males than for females.

Importantly, however, the most vital variable affecting future earnings for both men and women is not education but occupation, meaning the industry they work in or the type of position they hold or both. But this is particularly true for women. As indicated by the data, the most powerful variable influencing women's earnings is not a degree but successful pursuit of a career in high-paying occupations and industries.

TABLE 4.2 Variables Affecting Annual Earnings

Variable	Female Relative Importance	Male Relative Importance
College Preparatory	4.06	8.35
Vocational Education	4.66	7.97
Total Academic Credit	*	.77
Upper Socioeconomic Status	*	6.69
Married	−8.85	16.53
Divorced	*	15.68
College Graduate	5.57	7.31
Graduate School	16.37	20.24
Rural	−16.09	−13.22
Professional	17.147	15.78
Manager	29.02	23.99
Sales	*	26.55
Craft	*	7.51
Laborer	*	−15.11
Construction	14.68	6.94
Manufacturing	16.97	14.02
Communications	25.42	19.60
Entertainment	−21.76	−24.43
Public Administration	12.96	14.56

SOURCE: Gray and Huang (1991).
NOTE: * = no effect.

The importance of occupation in the gender wage gap issue is also illustrated in Table 4.1. It is noteworthy that although women are approaching parity in the Professional/Managerial ranks, women are less likely than men to be represented in high-paying professional occupations in manufacturing and in the skilled trades.

Only 4% of skilled craft workers are women (Noble, 1992). Thus, Terrell (1992) argues that narrowing the wage gap in the future will depend on breaking up sex segregation among occupations. Although some of the unequal representation of women in high-paying professional occupations may still have to do with gender barriers or so-called glass ceilings, in the case of many other high-paying occupations one major reason is that few women aspire to, and thus do not prepare for, these careers.

Women and Career Choice

Once, most young women may have anticipated that working in the home was to be their life work, but this is not the case today. An America Online poll (1998) found that 94% of young girls ages 8 to 18 viewed themselves as growing up to be career women. Female college freshmen are, in fact, slightly more likely than males to list "to be able to get a better job" as the number one reason for deciding to go to college. Yet, when it comes to the details, such as selecting a college major, females exhibit a high degree of stereotypical behavior.

Any doubt about the necessity for increased career maturity among young women graduating from high school should be dispelled by an examination of Table 4.3. The table lists the percentages of males and females, 92% of whom were either 18 or 19 years old, who indicated an intention to select various college majors. The distribution clearly demonstrates that traditional gender stereotypes regarding what are and are not appropriate careers for women have changed little. Women are five to eight times more likely to chose majors related to helping professions and less likely to choose majors in Engineering, Management, Computer Science, or nonprofessional Technical areas such as drafting, construction, or manufacturing. Importantly, virtually all majors that lead to high-skill/high-wage employment are dominated by men. Women still cluster in the low-paying professional occupations. It is also worth noting that women are 25% more likely to be undecided about careers.

Data provided in Table 4.3 suggest that, as a group, young women are both more likely to be undecided about college majors and, if they have decided, to select majors that lead to careers that are traditional for women and relatively low paying. Meanwhile, less than 10% of the workforce in careers that are high-skill/high-wage

TABLE 4.3 College Students' Intended Choice of Major, 1997 Entering Freshmen

Major	Men	Women
Male-Dominated Occupations		
Management	3.7%	1.8%
Electrical/Electronic Engineering	4.5%	0.5%
Mechanical Engineering	4.0%	0.3%
Technical (nonprofessional)	6.3%	1.4%
Computer Science	4.9%	1.6%
Female-Dominated Occupations		
Elementary Education	1.2%	8.4%
Nursing	0.4%	6.0%
Therapy	1.9%	5.0%
Psychology	1.8%	5.6%
Undecided	6.2%	8.4%

SOURCE: American Council on Education (1998).

and nontraditional for women are female. These realities have led researchers to argue that the socialization process of young women limits the options even considered by girls (Farmer, 1995). In general, males choose careers that are managerial, physical, mathematical, and/or scientific, whereas females choose careers in the helping professions (Kendall & Miller, 1993).

The stereotypical narrowing of career choices by girls happens by the middle school years. In one representative study of eighth graders, girls already showed a preference for careers in social services and the arts and an almost complete aversion to careers in technical and crafts areas (Bianchi, 1998). These stereotypes seem to stick. The typical profile of a woman who begins a career in a nontraditional area for women is 32 years old, divorced, with children

(Sternberg & Tuchscherer, 1992); this suggests that only economic necessity can break down these artificial barriers once they become established.

Women and Technical Careers

The classic case of gender-specific occupational stereotypes and their harmful effect has to do with the low number of women in information and other related technologies occupations, most of which are fast growing and high paying. The 1996 Current Population Survey conducted by the federal government found that only 28% of computer systems analysts and 31% of computer programmers were women even though 70% or more of these workers were younger than 44 years of age (U.S. Department of Commerce, 1998). Young women are three to four times less likely to major in electrical engineering or computer science and six times less likely to major in 2-year associate degree technical programs. At one major university noted for mathematics and science, 50% of women who enroll with the intention of majoring in science and engineering change colleges by the end of their freshman year. Only 17% of students taking the College Board Advanced Placement Test in computer science are female. The clues to this attitude can be traced to the early developmental years.

Women's attitudes toward technology in general and technical careers in particular can be traced to gender stereotypes adopted by teens, particularly in the junior high/middle school years. Swanson and Miller (1998) provide some interesting insight into this: Whereas boys and girls tend to perform about the same in mathematics, only 14% of girls say they are good in mathematics, compared with 22% of boys. Before the seventh grade, girls spend more time on computers than boys, but after that age the reverse is true. Only one quarter of teens using video games are girls; in video arcades, girls watch the boys play. These behaviors can be traced to a conventional, still dominant piece of "wisdom": Girls do not need to know much about technology outside that associated with homemaking; when they express negative attitudes toward technology and related academic disciplines, such as math and science, they are not discouraged. The opposite is true of boys.

Countering Gender Stereotyping

Women will never reach their true potential and thus will never reap their fair reward in the world of work until they themselves stop making limiting assumptions about what are or are not appropriate careers for women. Efforts to affect this process are most important in the early grades but particularly important in the middle school years. This is not to say that efforts cannot be effective with teens of high school age, but by then the task is to change attitudes already formed.

Involving parents is doubly important in efforts to erase limiting assumptions based on stereotypes. Writing in *Psychology of Women Quarterly,* Eccles (1994) argues that parents can affect career decisions either directly by agreeing to or withholding financial support or indirectly by encouraging or discouraging various career options. In one study of young women in Massachusetts, of the 61% who said they knew what careers they wanted to pursue, a high correlation was found between their choices and the occupations of their mothers. One dilemma that has emerged, however, is that parents, as a group, tend to endorse traditional gender occupational roles and to underestimate the talents of daughters while overestimating the talents of sons. In a survey in which parents reported what they wanted for their daughters (Roper Starch Worldwide, 1998), only 16% included "being a leader" and 11% "having a scientific mind." Also worth looking at are studies of women who have chosen to prepare for nontraditional careers and consistently report that parental support was the most important factor in making the choice (Sonoga, 1996).

On the positive side, the majority of parents today do understand the importance of their daughters having careers. The Roper study mentioned above did find that parents want their daughters to be self-reliant. The problem lies in the fact that parents still hold outdated ideas about women and work. Thus, changing this attitude is an important part of talking with parents.

Of course, many efforts and strategies are underway or are in place to counter occupational gender stereotyping. The national Take Your Daughters to Work Day is perhaps the best-known example. Some Internet resources that are useful in developing programs are listed in Table 4.4.

TABLE 4.4 Women and Work Web Sites (active as of January 1, 1999)

http://www.girltech.com	Provides information about gender equity in the area of technology and what adults can do to help
http://www.asem.org	Advocates for Women in Science, Engineering and Mathematics
http://www.aauw.org	American Association of University Women
http://www.girlsinc.org	Girls Incorporated
http://www.AnincomeOfherOwn.com	Independent Means
http://www.academic.org	Women's College Coalition
http://www.ywca.org	YWCA of the USA
http://www.womenwork.org	Nation Network/ Women's Employment

Racial Stereotypes

Although gender-specific occupational stereotypes receive significant national attention, equally destructive stereotypes exist with regard to determining appropriate careers by race. Such views are passed along to children during the socialization process and serve to limit occupational choice and, thus, opportunity. One example of this phenomenon is racial differences in the percentage of students reporting being encouraged to attend college and thus to pursue careers that require skills acquired at the postsecondary level (see Table 4.5).

Although attending college is not a career choice, it is an adequate proxy for professional/nonprofessional level of career aspiration. Thus, a good indicator of occupational stereotyping by race,

TABLE 4.5 Percentage of High School Sophomores Indicating Significant Adults Recommended College (1990)

Student Characteristics	Father	Mother	Guidance Counselor	Teacher
Male	77	83	65	66
Female	80	85	66	67
Asian	88	88	69	72
Hispanic	75	81	65	65
Black	69	77	66	70
White	78	84	65	65
American Indian	62	70	52	60
Low Socioeconomic Status	58	66	56	59
High Socioeconomic Status	95	98	78	76
Northeast	83	88	73	68
West	76	82	62	63
South	75	82	64	62

SOURCE: National Center for Education Statistics (1990).

socioeconomic status (SES), and region is differences in the percentage of youths who report that various adults have recommended they attend college. Such information is contained in Table 4.5. Where such advice occurs independently of stereotyping, no major differences should exist. Obviously, this is not the case. Of particular interest is the variance exhibited in the column for advice given by teachers; here, typical stereotypes emerge. Asians are viewed as academically gifted; Hispanics are not. And, reflecting the bias that the only hope for African Americans is to get a 4-year degree, teachers are the most likely to advise black students to go to college.

The Economically Disadvantaged

Efforts to promote career maturity are particularly important in promoting the opportunity and success of teens from disadvantaged homes, be they minority or majority students growing up in urban or rural areas. Providing opportunity to these young adults has been a persistent national goal, but success has been moderate. Of 1992 high school seniors, those in the low SES quartile were still half as likely (49%) to be enrolled in higher education as those in the highest quartile (91%). Only 19% of students in the low SES quartile were in 4-year colleges, compared with 70% of those in the highest. Data in Table 4.5 provide at least one reason: Teens from low SES are much less likely to report being encouraged to go to college.

Countering Stereotypes Encountered by the Disadvantaged

Countering stereotypes encountered by the disadvantaged is important, complex, and difficult. Yet, a key strategy—perhaps *the* key strategy—is helping these youths develop career goals. Although well intended, programs designed solely to increase college enrollment of disadvantaged youths without efforts to help them develop commensurate goals for matriculating lead to the same results as it does for majority youths—failure. Fisher and Griggs's (1995) study of successful black and Hispanic students found that the factor most frequently indicated by students as responsible for their success was being goal oriented, which they defined as having a specific career goal. These findings are consistent with others (e.g., Educational Testing Service, 1989) that found "early" career decisions to be consistent predictors of postsecondary success among students from low-SES homes. As suggested by Fisher and Griggs, being career oriented allows students to remain focused. This focus must be developed prior to high school graduation. Schools were found to have played an important role in this development by providing role models, encouragement, and opportunities to develop and verify career directions. Importantly, students in the Fisher and Griggs study reported that internship experiences were very important in developing career focus and should be provided in high school.

Of course, many efforts and strategies are also underway or in place to counter stereotypes faced by disadvantaged youths. An excellent place to start an exploration of such efforts is, again, the Internet. Typically, such sites have links to other sites not listed. Two Internet resources useful in developing programs are http:// www.math.buffalo.edu/mad/mad0.html (history of, and opportunities for, African Americans in mathematics) and http://www.lib.lsu.edu/lib/chem/display/faces.html (history of, and opportunities for, African Americans in science).

Regional Isolation

Finally, harmful narrowing of career choices may be attributable to the region in which students grow up. Both rural and inner-city America provide little in terms of positive and/or diverse exposure to career opportunities. Although this is not stereotyping in the typical sense, it has the same effect—namely, to limit opportunity by limiting choice. For this reason, career maturity/career development efforts in these locales must take into account the necessity of getting students to look beyond what they see in their towns or neighborhoods.

Promoting Success

Although post-high-school success depends on both skill and focus, maximizing each student's human potential requires that occupational choices not be narrowed by stereotypical views regarding work as it relates to gender, race, ethnicity, SES, or geographic region. In the extreme, such stereotypes leave teens with a sense of hopelessness. In all cases, the result is a limiting of choices under consideration.

Most occupational stereotypes are learned by students during their school years; thus, schools have important potential for counteracting this process. Doing so is not easy; often, parents themselves are the source of such stereotypes. Also, too often what seems possible to students is defined by the communities they grow up in or the income level of their homes. Thus, helping teens "get real" includes helping them get beyond their limiting assumptions as based on their gender, race, economic situation at home, or where they live.

Part 2

Strategies
to Promote
Career Direction

When the goal is postsecondary success, two types of maturity are required: academic and career. One sign of academic maturity is appropriate levels of academic skills; one sign of career maturity is an appropriate level of career direction. Even though parents, schools, and the nation have always focused on academic maturity, career maturity has not been viewed as important. Yet, for this generation, both are crucial. Both are directly related to success or failure. The purpose of Part 2 is to look at strategies for promoting postsecondary success by increasing career awareness and improving decision making. In Chapter 5, the concept of career maturity is explored and strategies are discussed. Chapter 6 presents a variety of alternatives for students to take after high school in order to reach their career goals, including the old-fashioned idea of taking a year to mature. And perhaps most important, Chapter 7 involves working with parents and the business community. Chapter 8 is a summary chapter.

Fostering Career Maturity and Direction

Although getting a good job is the expressed goal of graduating high school seniors, few can fill in the details. A mature teenager can. Does it matter? Yes, for this generation it does matter. There is not enough high-skill/high-wage employment to go around. Those who will be successful in competing for these jobs will be those with relevant skills. These skills will give them an advantage over all the others in line for the same jobs. Developing these skills requires a decision about a career or related group of jobs to prepare to compete for. *Career maturity* is the developmental state that enables teens to make these decisions. This chapter begins with a discussion of what, according to researchers, leads to a successful career and thus what variables teens should consider when making career decisions. Next, the specific attributes of adolescent career maturity are explained; these attributes should be the outcome goals of career development programs. The chapter then goes on to discuss various strategies to promote career maturity and direction.

What Leads to Career Success?

For most teens, success in life includes having a successful career. But what is known about career success that will help teens make better decisions? There are two main theories. One is the "trait/factor" approach. Specifically, a person's success in any particular career depends on a good match between that person's aptitudes, abilities, and temperament and the skill set and culture of the occupation. In the trait/factor approach, the goal is to find the one or more careers that are the best fit. Individuals are successful in careers that require what they are good at and where the culture of the job fits their temperaments. In this approach, career decision making hinges on matching an individual skill and aptitude with those of various occupations. The use of tests such as the Differential Aptitude Test, tests given by the Armed Forces, and the new Work Keys instrument are based on this approach.

A second theory can be thought of as the "implementing a self-concept" approach. In this case, success in a chosen career is viewed as resulting more from the degree to which the career is consistent with an individual's self-concept or the mental picture the person has of him- or herself as a person—values, likes, and dislikes. The idea is that an individual will make the effort necessary to succeed (regardless of the match or mismatch between an occupation's skill set and culture) if the career is consistent with how the person views him- or herself or how the person wants to be viewed by others. In this case, success is believed to result from the degree to which a person is employed in an occupation the person "feels" is suitable. Whereas the trait/factor approach hinges on an accurate perception of one's skills and aptitudes, the self-concept approach hinges on knowing oneself. Holland's Self-Directed Search (Holland, 1994) is one example of a career development instrument based on this theory of career success.

The position taken in this book is that both theories are correct. On the one hand, the degree to which an occupation agrees with a person's self-concept will determine how happy the person is. On the other hand, the degree to which the skill set and culture of an occupation are consistent with the aptitudes, skills, and temperament of an individual will probably determine how successful the person is. Both are important. Evidence, both research and anecdotal, suggests the validity of this conclusion. The hope or dream of many teens is to be a teacher, yet when the time comes, they find that they lack a complex skill set needed to be successful. Likewise, many who have the skill set to be successful are unhappy because their work is inconsistent with the reality they seek—thus the finding that 60% of individuals in professional high-wage careers report that they would do something different if they could.

Characteristics of
Effective Career Decisions

From the previous discussions regarding what predicts career success, it is clear that effective career decisions are based on both a good match between a person's self-concept and his or her hopes, dreams, and abilities. Therefore, effective career planning requires the willingness to look objectively at "all" the factors. Such a willingness is an attribute of career maturity. What teens want to be is important, but success requires that it be tempered with the realities of what they are good at and finally, of course, the labor market outlook for employment and thus the competition.

Currently, many teens make no career decisions at all. They go to college by default: They do not know what else to do. Helping them get to the point where they start making postsecondary decisions based on what they would like to do is a step forward. But without a willingness to deal with the realities of their aptitudes, skills, and temperaments, these decisions will still have a relatively low probability of success.

Career Maturity in Adolescence

Some behaviors indicate a teen's readiness to develop a career direction and to make plans to pursue this interest (Herr & Cramer, 1996; Super, 1977, 1985). These behaviors are collectively termed *career maturity*. Research suggests that these behaviors predict whether an individual will have a stable success career path or flounder. These behaviors become the student's outcome goals of curricular, program, and instructional design to promote career maturity and direction.

Table 5.1 presents an adaptation of the work of both Super (1977, 1985) and Herr and Cramer (1996). It divides career maturity attributes into three groups. The first group is understanding that planning is important and that planning requires the willingness to face reality. The second group is a set of academic/interpersonal skills one must master to make and implement effective career plans. The third group is knowing oneself enough to be able to project likes and dislikes into career choices.

TABLE 5.1 Career Mature Behavior for Adolescents

I. ATTITUDES
- Appreciation for the importance of planning
- Willingness to face reality

II. SKILLS
- Career exploration skills
- Decision-making skills

III. KNOWLEDGE OF SELF
- Understanding of self in relation to the world of work

I. Career-Mature Attitudes: Appreciation for the Importance of Planning

The fundamental attitude of a career-mature person is a belief that planning improves the likelihood of success. It begins with the "inner directed" attitude that life's fortunes are not just a question of luck, but of one's actions, and that actions are most effective if planned. It is grounded in a more fundamental attitude known as hope. Teens who see no hope will also see no reason to plan. Also, some teens have the idea that going to college is a plan; it isn't. College is a means to an end. Only when going to college is a part of a plan does it become a means to an end. Can these attitudes be taught? Yes! Instruction designed to promote a commitment to planning should have some of the following student outcome goals:

- Understanding that life is not futile, that planning is not futile
- Being aware of the need to have a postsecondary plan
- Understanding that college is not an end in itself
- Understanding immediate versus intermediate choices

I. Career-Mature Attitudes: Willingness to Face Reality

A second fundamental attitude of a career-mature teen is the willingness to face reality. Getting teens to face reality may be the most difficult task in career development efforts. First, many will have parents who are not ready to face reality. In fact, the majority of today's teens grew up in an environment that strives to protect them from reality. Make-believe sports leagues for children, social promotions, and grade inflation for teens are examples of shielding youths from reality. Colleges and universities are part of the problem as well; many such institutions admit that the students they know cannot do real college-level academics. Also, for some teens, "getting real" means making plans that may differ from the norm. Yet, if the goal is success, dealing with reality is fundamental. Experiences designed to help youths face reality should focus on helping youths address such issues as those listed below:

Willingness to evaluate
- Their level of academic interest
- Their high school grades
- Their college entrance scores
- Their level of career focus
- Their readiness for life away from home

All these topics are wake-up calls for students and parents, signaling that some postsecondary plans may or may not lead to success. The number of teens who hated school for 12 years but still go to college is amazing. Even among those who have always liked academics, have good grades and college board scores, and have career directions, some are still not ready to leave home. As long as teens are unwilling to face these realities, many will graduate from high school and head off to college and failure.

II. Career-Mature Skills:
Career Exploration Skills

Career-mature persons know how to conduct ongoing personal career exploration. They have been exposed to techniques of personal career exploration. When they are exposed to different careers, they automatically visualize themselves in those particular occupations. They know something about labor markets, labor market projections, and sources of labor market information. They are not experts, but they are at least savvy consumers. In particular, they have been taught how to explore career options that appeal to them. Career exploration skills include the following:

- How to acquire information regarding careers
- How to verify tentative career interests
- How to identify options for preparation for career interests

II. Career-Mature Skills: Decision-Making Skills

The statement "I can't decide" is all too familiar to parents and educators. The typical reaction is to conclude that the individual saying it has insufficient background or has had insufficient time to evaluate the information. It could be, however, that the individual does not know how to go about making a decision. It is a mistake to assume that teens know how to make decisions. Depending on individual differences, decision making can be very difficult. Individuals whose preferred style is to deal with life by "doing what feels right" may find themselves stymied when nothing or everything feels right. These individuals need to be taught logical decision making.

Furthermore, it is important to remember that career decision making is unique; both the variables involved and the consequences that include selecting an appropriate college. Career decision making is a process of evaluating one's self-concept and the realities of one's aptitudes, abilities, and temperament, with like factors associated with various careers. Career decision-making skills include the following:

1. Developing decision-making strategies
2. Understanding the importance of having a fallback plan
3. Understanding that successful career decisions come from matching aptitudes, abilities, and hopes and dreams with opportunities in the labor market
4. Understanding how to interpret labor market information

Effective career decision-making skills are gained as follows: First, teens develop decision-making strategies or processes that they can apply to this and other situations down the road. Second, they gain an understanding of the importance of having a Plan A and a Plan B and of having the courage to "get real" about when Plan B should become Plan A. Third, they gain an understanding that success and happiness stem from choosing careers that meet their personal expectations for themselves, their skills, and their aptitudes to learn new skills, all of which are tempered by labor market realities of supply and demand. Finally, they acquire the skills to be savvy consumers of labor market information.

III. Knowledge of Self: Understanding of Self in Relation to the World of Work

If career success and happiness depend on a good match between a person's self-concept—the type of person he or she is—and what the person hopes to achieve, then "knowing oneself" is crucial. It is also very difficult, but it is not impossible. This is not the stuff of psychoanalysis or "T" groups, but of thinking about relatively low-risk introspective/reflective questions such as "When I think of myself working, what am I wearing? Is it inside or outside?" and so on. It is also knowing one's strengths and weaknesses, which is not easy either. Very often, a weakness is explained away, particularly by parents, as resulting from lack of effort. Often, lack of effort is the result of lack of ability; most people find success a good motivator.

Knowledge of self for teens also includes an honest appraisal of maturity and motivation. A particular postsecondary plan may be a great plan, but the question that is most important to ask is "Am I ready now?" For example, students whose achievements to date have been attributable more to domineering parents may not be ready for the independence of a college campus hundreds of miles away from Mom and Dad and the structure they provide. Of course, knowledge of oneself is a lifelong process, or as the saying goes, "If I only knew then what I now know about myself." This is not a reason for teens not to reflect on their experience to date as a way to make better postsecondary plans. Career-mature teens should do the following:

- Reflect on the mental pictures they have of themselves at work
- Reflect on their academic aptitudes, levels of skills, and interests
- Reflect on their readiness or maturity to prepare for a career

In this section of the chapter, the behavioral characteristics of adolescent career maturity are discussed. This list is useful in citing student outcome goals and in guiding efforts to promote overall career maturity. Several points are worth emphasizing. First, career maturity requires a commitment to planning that, in turn, is rooted in a sense of hope. Children who do not have hope do not see a need to plan. Second, many teens and many parents are not willing to face reality, pain, and conflict. This does not mean that efforts to improve teen career maturity are destined to fail but that designers and implementers should begin at the beginning, with the prerequisite attitudes about planning and reality (see Chapter 7 regarding parents). Also keep in mind that these behaviors are interrelated. Knowledge of self cannot be gained without a willingness to "get real," and why "get real" if there is no hope and/or need to?

Strategies to Promote Adolescent Career Maturity and Direction

We turn now to a discussion of the various strategies that can be employed to foster career maturity and career direction among teens. Before moving on to this discussion, however, it seems wise to restate the overall goal: postsecondary success. Exactly what is it we are trying to achieve? The following are the three specific goals:

1. By the 10th grade, all students will have participated in activities designed to help them identify several tentative career interests to prepare for after high school.

2. In the 11th and 12th grades, all students will participate in activities that allow them to verify or reject these choices, using the results to develop postsecondary plans.

3. All students will graduate with postsecondary plans that have a high probability of success and that will enable them to realize their hopes and dreams.

In the light of the goals listed above, strategies to promote career maturity can be divided into two groups: (a) those targeted toward helping students reach tentative career directions by the 10th grade and (b) opportunities to verify these experiences in the last 2 years of high school in order to develop a postsecondary plan.

Goal 1: Promoting a Tentative Career Direction While in the 10th Grade

The first major student outcome goal in career development efforts is to enable students to identify possible career option on which to focus during the last 2 years of high school. This goal should be the terminal outcome of all K-10 career development efforts.

The 10th grade is an important "choice point" in student academic preparation, a time when students can make final selections of programs of study and courses in high school. Academic programs such as tech prep, honors, and vocational education most often begin in the junior year. The goal is to help students develop tentative career motives for making these curriculum and course selection decisions. The most effective programs toward achieving this end are comprehensive in nature. Two of the most prominent types of school-based programs are individual career plans and career majors/pathways.

Individual Career Plans

The *individual career plan (ICP)*, as the name suggests, is an actual document/portfolio/folder a student develops as part of a comprehensive career development program (see Gray & Herr, 1995, p. 116). Typically, this plan is developed in the junior high/middle school years and serves as a basis for course selection in the 9th or 10th grade. The ICP is a joint venture between student and parents, who are asked to review it and, often, to sign it. The ICP, when required as a condition for high school course selection, is an excellent way to bring relevance to elementary and especially middle or junior high school career development efforts: Knowing that an ICP is required for high school course selection, most students take seriously the educational programs/courses leading up to it.

Another important aspect of the ICP is the expectation that students and parents will review them periodically at prescribed times established by the high school. In some high schools, a student/parent/teacher conference to review the ICP is a requirement for course selection each year. While predictable, many high school freshmen will still exhibit various levels of fantasy regarding post-secondary plans; the ICP provides a vehicle for structuring time for reality checks as the student progresses. Thus, the ICP is among the best approaches to structuring a time when teens—and parents—must face reality: They may choose to ignore the wake-up calls, but they cannot avoid facing them if an updated ICP is a requirement for yearly course selection.

Career Pathways/Career Majors/ Career Academics

Perhaps the most comprehensive and ambitious efforts to develop career maturity among teens involve adding career majors or pathways to the high school program of study. West Virginia, for example, requires all students to select career majors by the 10th grade. Typically, *career pathways* are large occupational clusters. Within each of these large clusters are career majors. Each major is subdivided into professional, skilled, and entry-level occupations (see Table 5.2).

Each student is required to choose a career major or pathway. Making this choice is the focus of a comprehensive career development program in the preceding grades. In larger high schools with more scheduling and course options, different academic programs of study are developed for each occupational level with each major. In smaller high schools, the number of majors is typically four (e.g., engineering/industrial, health/science & human services, business technology, and arts/humanities). In these smaller high schools, developing many programs of study may not be realistic. Instead, then, programs such as tech prep are used to provide a focused academic sequence for those interested in preparing for 2-year technical education. Career majors become the focus of career verification efforts in the junior and senior years.

Perhaps the most important aspect of ICP and career majors/ pathways lies in the message it sends to students and parents—namely, that career maturity and career focus are crucial to success. The objective of these efforts is not to vocationalize the curriculum nor to take decision making out of the hands of families, but instead to promote postsecondary success by helping teens and parents make better decisions.

TABLE 5.2 Career Major/Pathway Format

Career Cluster: Engineering/Technical
Career Major: Manufacturing Production Technology

Career Options

Professional Level	Skilled Level	Entry Level
Industrial Engineer	Industrial Engineer Technician	Welder
Mechanical Engineer	Industrial Maintenance Technician	Sheetmetal Worker
Quality Engineer	Drafting Technician	Electrician

SOURCE: West Virginia Department of Education.

Career Academies

The most comprehensive model of education reform designed to promote both academic and career maturity is career academies. A *career academy* is an entire self-contained academic unit focused around a career cluster, such as health or information technology. Career academies are found primarily in urban centers or large districts that have multiple high schools, providing the opportunity to designate one or more a career magnet. It is possible, however, to establish a career academy with a large high school in much the same way large high schools have established various houses or schools within a school. In the career academy approach, the occupational cluster becomes the context for academics as well as skill building. Often, they are sponsored directly by related industries.

Goal 2: Verifying Tentative Career Directions

The second outcome goal of career development efforts is to provide opportunities for teens to verify tentative decisions made on career interests by the 10th grade. The objective is to verify these decisions by observing or, even better, working in the occupation, be it paid employment or internships. The intent is to reduce the number of incidents in which students suddenly discover in college that they do not like their major and elect to change it.

School-to-Work

Perhaps the most comprehensive effort to connect students with the world of work is the federal school-to-work (STW) effort. Initially designed to provide a better transition system for those who pursue full-time employment after high school graduation, it changed its focus quickly from school-to-work to school-to-career. The program's new intent is to provide an opportunity for teens to crystallize tentative career interests via school-sponsored work-based experience. Thus, for most teens, STW(C) programs are providing opportunities to verify tentative career decisions as a basis for postsecondary planning. Typically, the work-based component of the program takes one of the following forms, all of which are good ways for youths to verify their career interests as a prerequisite to successful postsecondary planning.

Career Verification Activities

- Paid related part-time work experience
- Summer work experience
- Community-based internships
- School system internships
- Volunteerism
- School-based enterprises
- Job shadowing
- Interviewing incumbent workers
- Workplace site observations
- School-sponsored career seminars
- Community-sponsored career speakers bureau

Goal 3: Developing a Postsecondary Plan

The final outcome goal for teens is to develop a postsecondary plan that has a high probability of success. Such a plan should be a logical extension of verification experiences that also take place in the last 2 years of high school. The planning process involves a matching of career interests, aptitudes and achievements, and maturity with various options (see Chapter 6). This type of planning requires individual attention and the involvement of teachers.

The challenge for high school educators is how to provide this individual attention in the light of high student-to-staff ratios. Although the consensus may have been that this type of counseling is the duty of guidance personnel, most settings have just too few counselors, compared to the size of the student body. Another approach is the faculty adviser concept.

The Faculty Adviser System

Colleges and universities have counseling offices, and yet every student has a different faculty adviser. At the college level, advising is viewed as a faculty responsibility. The same model has been applied in some high schools. Each member of the professional staff becomes an adviser to a group of students. This adviser becomes the first point of contact for each student's parents and the school. In some high schools, course selection requires each student and his or her parents or guardians to meet with the adviser as a prerequisite to enrolling for the next year and thus fits nicely with the individual career plan model. The overall goal of the faculty adviser is to help each advisee develop, over the 4 years of high school, a postsecondary plan focusing on the year after graduation.

In high schools that have adopted the faculty adviser system, guidance and counseling staff advise faculty and act as a source of referral for students facing unique challenges. Guidance counselors have groups of advisees, like all faculty, but they are also responsible for providing faculty with the information the teachers need to be effective advisers and other details that need attention.

The Graduation Portfolio

Should a student's postsecondary plan be a written document? In schools that have adopted the individual career plan (ICP) format, the answer is a given. Schools that have not adopted this system have a second option—namely, requiring a graduation portfolio as a condition of graduation. Some states require such a portfolio. A *portfolio* typically is a collection of things that demonstrate what an individual can do versus what the individual knows. When used as a career planning strategy, the portfolio becomes a demonstration of what a student can do in the light of his or her career interests and postsecondary plan.

Comprehensive Career Guidance Programs

In many high schools, the lead responsibility for career development/career maturity efforts is taken by guidance professionals who design and, in most cases, deliver comprehensive career guidance programs. According to the American School Counselors Association (ASCA), school counseling programs should facilitate student development in three areas: academic development, career development, and personal development (Campbell & Dahir, 1997). Considering that the average student-to-counselor ratio in public high schools is 330 to 1, individual counseling to achieve student development in these three areas is not very realistic. Thus, some guidance professionals have adopted a curricular approach to providing these important services: Comprehensive career guidance is one curriculum effort. ASCA standards for career development efforts are drawn from the literature regarding career maturity—specifically, National Standards for School Counseling Programs as described below (from Campbell & Dahir, 1997, p. 24):

National Standards for School
Counseling Career Development Programs

- Standard A: Students will acquire the skills to investigate the world of work in relation to knowledge of self and to make informed career decisions.
- Standard B: Students will employ strategies to achieve future career success and satisfaction.

- Standard C: Students will understand the relationship among personal qualities, education and training, and the world of work.

The competencies listed for each of the three standards would well serve any group interested in career development/career maturity efforts. School counselors are typically among the few professionals with formal training in career development theory and practices, and they are also typically crucial elements in success efforts. Recognizing the crucial nature of the school counselor in providing a link between students and their chances for rewarding careers, the National Center for Research in Vocational Education (NCRVE) conducts a yearly competition to recognize exemplary guidance and counseling programs that, in turn, serve as valuable resources for those starting such programs (Cunanan & Maddy-Bernstein, 1997).

Career Assessment Materials

A variety of published materials are available to help students develop career direction. Of particular interest are the more than 300 different psychological instruments available that are designed to provide information on making individual career choices. These instruments can be categorized into two types: interests/values (e.g., Self-Directed Search) and aptitudes/achievements (e.g., Work Keys). Some comprehensive instruments provide both types of information (for a complete guide, see Kapes, Mastie, & Whitefield, 1988).

Many of these instruments, particularly the new comprehensive instruments, are excellent. They also represent a significant dollar investment for most districts. Thus, a word of caution is offered: Career assessment instruments are excellent *as part of* a career development program, but they are typically not effective when used as a stand-alone activity. The information's usefulness is related to the student's readiness to use it. Thus, activities that precede the assessment and their outcomes are crucial. Typically, however, a district will give an interest assessment in isolation as part of its testing program. Although perhaps better than nothing, this shot-in-the-dark approach is typically not effective with most students.

A wealth of career development materials is also on the market today. Some of these are designed to assist students in conducting career searches; others provide career information that may be used as part of a search. Increasingly, such materials are computer based and/or Internet based (see Table 5.3). Reviewing such materials would fill a book. Most guidance and school-to-work staff are excellent resources for selecting such materials. Again, however, such materials are effective only to the degree that they are part of an overall instructional program.

The Academic Program and Career Direction

Postsecondary success is a function of both academic and career maturity. This dichotomy does not mean that career maturity efforts should avoid academic subjects or, more important, that academic subjects should not be connected to careers. Of the professionals encountered by students in the classroom, teachers dominate in terms of contact time and thus influence. Academic faculty have a crucial voice in the "get real" message. Academic teachers also can be important in helping students develop both career maturity and career direction if they choose to do so. Data from the National Center for Education Statistics (NCES) suggest that about two thirds of teachers do take time to try to link their subjects to the real world (see Table 5.4).

The point to be made is that academic teachers have a vital role to play in career maturity/career development programs. If schools elect to start a faculty adviser program, academic teachers will be the majority of advisers because, on a time basis alone, they have the most contact with students. Thus, academic faculty can serve a vital role in dispelling workforce misconceptions. Schools that adopt career majors/pathways cannot develop unique courses of study without involving academic teachers; it simply will not work without their support. Faculty who work with students from the academic middle should link their content to the world of work to improve learning. The research is clear in this regard: Most students learn when the content is put into a context they can relate to.

Tech Prep

One specific academic program, tech prep, deserves special mention in that it is both an academic and a career development program. The student outcome goal of the program is the transition from high school to pre-bachelor's degree technical education. The

TABLE 5.3 Internet Resources

AMERICA JOB BANK: http://www.ajb.dni.us
  U.S. Department of Labor link to 1,800 local state
  employment service programs

CAREER MAGAZINE: http://www. careermag.com
  On-line career information resource

CAREER MOSAIC: http://www.careermosaic.com
  Includes a career resource center

CAREER NET: http://www.career.org
  Includes a directory to other Web career sources

ERISS: http://www.eriss.com/jobseek.htm
  Listing of job search software and Web sites

CATAPULT, THE NATIONAL ASSOCIATION OF COLLEGES
  AND EMPLOYERS: http://www.jobweb.org/catapult/
 catapult.htm
    References to career guides, professional associations,
    and college career centers

COLLEGE VIEW: http://www.collegeview.com
  Information on 2- and 4-year colleges, including Web sites

PETERSON'S EDUCATION CENTER: http://www.petersons.com
  Sections on distance learning, testing and assessment,
  and vocational technical schools

MICROSOFT'S AUTHORIZED ACADEMIC TRAINING
  PROGRAM: http://www.microsoft.com

SOURCE: American Vocational Education Association (1997).

program of study is tailored to this end and typically includes applied mathematics and science courses. *Tech prep* is an effort to develop a structured academic program for students in the academic middle who are in the college prep program of study and have tentative career interests that require postsecondary technical educa-

TABLE 5.4 Percentage of Teachers Who Link Academics to the Real World

K-8	73%
Science	67%
Social Studies	67%
Vocational Education	63%
English	60%
Mathematics	49%

SOURCE: National Center for Education Statistics (1997).

tion. As such, tech prep is a program within the college prep program. Enrolling in tech prep requires decisions by students and parents that are similar to those in selecting career majors/pathways. Tech prep programs are usually developed to prepare students to transition to unique types of postsecondary pre-bachelor's degree education, such as allied health, manufacturing technology, and engineering technology. Thus, enrolling in tech prep implies that a student has made some tentative career decisions. Quite often, the tech prep curriculum includes instruction and experiences to assist students in making this decision.

Promoting Success

When the goal is postsecondary success, both academic and career maturity or direction become important. Lack of commitment is as much a source of postsecondary failure as poor academic skills. Commitment comes from having career direction. This chapter provided specific student learning outcomes for career development efforts for teens. All too often, efforts to promote career maturity fail because of a failure to state exactly the desired outcome. The following three goals are recommended: (a) By the 10th grade, students should have developed tentative career interests; (b) these interests serve as the focus for career verification experiences in the 11th and 12th grades, which, in turn, (c) serve to focus the development and initial implementation of a postsecondary plan. A variety of strategies were introduced that have been used across the country to achieve this end. The postsecondary plan itself identifies what a student will do after high school to achieve career goals. Of course, many options are available, only one of which is bachelor's degree education. Exploring these options is the topic of Chapter 6.

Chapter 6

Considering All the Alternatives

Postsecondary success for all teens requires academic and career maturity. Career maturity enables a teen to develop and verify career goals that provide direction or a purpose for post-high-school pursuits. Once career goals have been developed, a final and crucial element in a postsecondary plan is to consider all the alternatives for developing the skills necessary to gain entry to the chosen occupational field. Currently, the majority of teens and parents think there is only one alternative—namely, bachelor's degree education. Of course, for those teens with (a) advanced academic skills, (b) verified career interests that require a bachelor's degree, and (c) the ability to live away from home, such a goal is the right one. The rest probably have better alternatives. The purpose of this chapter is to discuss alternatives, including taking a year off.

Traditional Bachelor's Degree

The post-high-school alternative that needs little explanation is a bachelor's degree, or 4-year college education. National surveys indicate that 85% of today's teens indicate this as a goal, with about one third expressing an intent to pursue graduate education afterward. Their hope is that this course of action will ultimately lead to a career in the professions. For some it will, but for most it will not.

At best, half will graduate from college in 6 years; of those who do, only 57 commensurate jobs will be available for every 100 degrees awarded. Thus, the success rate will be about 25% to 30% for an experience that will cost at least $45,000, and even more, a great deal more.

I can think of many good reasons to encourage youths at least to consider alternatives to a 4-year college education. Ultimately, the decision is theirs and their parents' to make, but they also deserve to be informed. The approach advocated in this book involves a process that develops a career direction that will lead to focused postsecondary plans and to better planning or decisions, contributing ultimately to a higher probability of success. Even when this process leads to bachelor's degree education, however, teens and parents need to recognize a "few" realities, beginning with the low number of high school graduates actually prepared for college-level work.

Nationwide assessments of academic skills, such as the National Assessment of Educational Progress (NAEP), suggest that only 40%, at best, graduate from high school with the academic skills to do real college-level academics. Because only a few hundred of the nation's 4-year colleges admit 70% or more of all applicants, having poor academic skills is no longer a barrier to getting into a 4-year college; however, it is still a barrier to graduation. Students who graduate from high school without completing mathematics through Algebra II, taking 2 years of the same foreign language, taking two laboratory sciences, and having a B average and combined SAT scores of 1,100 or ACT 22 are at risk. The Higher Education Research Institute reports that students who enter college with a C average are six times more likely to drop out as those with an A average. Those with combined SAT scores of 800 or less are three times less likely to graduate than those with scores of 1,000 or better (Gray & Herr, 1996).

A second reality is remedial education in college. Parents assume that college admission is an indication of qualification for college work. No! Today's colleges admit students that they themselves have determined are not able to do college-level academic work. The National Association of Development Educators, composed of faculty who teach remedial courses, claims that one in two students who enters college needs remedial work in English, mathematics, or science (Gray & Herr, 1996).

The major problem with remedial education is that although it is effective for adults who are returning to college, it is not effective for teens who have just graduated from high school: in fact, for teens it indicates that they are unlikely to graduate. Researchers at the Fordham Foundation (www.edexcellence.net) concluded that although the intent of remedial education is to improve access to higher education, the result has been to lower the overall percentage of graduates.

Another reality is that not all colleges enjoy equal status in the labor market. Students with poor academic records get into 4-year colleges but not the better ones. Add to this the reality that students with poor academic records are also the least likely to be admitted to the most promising and sought-after college majors, and it is clear that even if poorly prepared college students persist to graduation, their reward will probably be underemployment. They would be better off considering alternatives.

The final reality is that the occupational outlook for jobs requiring a 4-year degree is dismal (a point reiterated often in this book). Again, the U.S. Department of Labor projects 57 university-level jobs for every 100 students who earn a college degree. The information in Table 6.1 is one indication of this reality. Based on an NCES study of 11,000 college graduates during the 1992-93 academic year, the data indicate the percentage of graduates who, 1 year later, said they were employed in jobs that required a 4-year degree. In general, about half so indicated.

Bachelor's Degrees in Technology

One little-known gem among 4-year college majors is a bachelor's degree in technology. Unlike engineering degrees, these programs are typically more applied and more specific. Whereas engineering degrees are bookish, technology degrees are hands-on. An excellent example of these programs may be found at the University of Wisconsin–Stout (www.uwstout.edu/ugbull/ugbcontents.html) or Pennsylvania State University at Altoona and Barren (www.psu.edu). UW–Stout, for example, offers four degree programs in more than 10 technical areas ranging from the common (e.g., construction, manufacturing & industrial technology) to the uncommon (e.g., packaging, apparel design/manufacturing, tele-

TABLE 6.1 Percentage of 1992 College Graduates Who Indicated They Held a Job 1 Year Later That Requires a 4-Year Degree

Major	Commensurate Employment
All Graduates	56%
Biological Science	49%
Business	51%
Education	66%
Engineering	79%
Health Professions	73%
History	41%
Humanities	45%
Mathematics/Computer Science	68%
Psychology	45%
Social Sciences	47%

SOURCE: National Center for Education Statistics (1993).

communications systems). These degrees are gems because graduates are highly sought-after by employers and paid well because, unlike graduates of engineering programs, these graduates know how to do things relevant to employers' core businesses. In fact, many college engineering programs are beginning to copy the applied or hands-on content of technology courses to increase the competitiveness of their graduates in the labor market.

Pre-Bachelor's Degree Postsecondary Technical Education

To the detriment of both teens and the nation, college is most frequently identified with bachelor's degrees and graduate education. Thus, just as the labor market opportunities in nonprofessional high-skill/high-wage careers are largely unknown, so too are the opportunities in postsecondary technical education below the bachelor's degree level. Somewhat ironically, the main public provider of this type of education, community colleges, often takes on this mission reluctantly, preferring instead the less expensive role of being a less costly alternative transfer route to a 4-year degree. Prebachelor's degrees in the technologies take three forms: associate degree in engineering technology (AET), associate degree of applied science (AAS), and certificate programs.

Associate Degree in Engineering Technology (AET)

An associate degree in engineering technology (AET) may be regarded as very similar to a 4-year technology degree without the general education and theory. Such degree programs are often offered by universities that also have 4-year engineering and/or technology programs. Although these programs are not designed for transfer to a 4-year college program, typically they are articulated with 4-year technology degrees. An important characteristic (and one that students and parents should be aware of) is that they are accredited by the Accrediting Board for Engineering and Technology (ABET). A list of all ABET accredited programs is available at its Web site (www.abet.org/tac/TACWebsite.html). Table 6.2 contains a typical list of AET programs.

Associate Degree of Applied Science (AAS)

An associate degree of applied science (AAS) is typically offered in areas not associated with engineering, such as the health fields and food service. An excellent example of the variety of such degree programs may be seen at the Penn College of Technology Web site (www.penncollege.edu). AAS degrees typically are even more applied or hands-on than AET degrees and require less advanced mathematics and science. Table 6.3 contains examples of AAS programs.

TABLE 6.2 AET Degree Programs

Architectural Engineering Technology

Automatic Control Chemical Engineering Technology

Chemical Engineering Technology

Building Environmental Systems Technology

Biomedical Engineering Technology

Chemical Engineering Technology

Civil Engineering Technology

Computer Engineering Technology

Construction Chemical Engineering Technology

Electrical Engineering Technology

Electronics Engineering Technology

Environmental Systems Engineering Technology

Industrial Engineering Technology

Laser Engineering Technology

Manufacturing Engineering Technology

Mechanical Engineering Technology

Plastic/Polymer Engineering Technology

Surveying Engineering Technology

Telecommunications Engineering

Certificate Programs

Of the 10,246 institutions providing higher education in the United States, 6,558 award certificates, not degrees. Certificate programs are the most occupation specific and take the shortest time to complete. Neither of these qualities makes them any less attractive. In many cases, certificates are offered by institutions that offer associate degrees in the same occupation; the only difference is that the latter requires general education courses. If the goal is to acquire specific skills that will provide a labor market advantage as quickly as

TABLE 6.3 AAS Degree Programs

COMPUTER TECHNOLOGIES
    Business Program Emphasis
    Microcomputer Specialist

HEALTH
    Cardiovascular Technology
    Dental Hygiene
    Surgical Technology

HOSPITALITY
    Baking & Pastry Arts
    Culinary Arts
    Food & Hospitality Management

INDUSTRIAL/MANUFACTURING TECHNOLOGY
    Quality Assurance Technology
    Toolmaking Technology
    Welding Technology
    Wood Products Technology

TRANSPORTATION
    Aviation Technology
    Diesel Technology

possible, a certificate program is ideal. The following are examples of certificate programs: Computer Applications, Electrical Occupations, Heavy Construction Equipment Technician, Practical Nurse, and Plumbing.

Transferability

For good reason, both teens and parents are often concerned about the possibility of continuing on for a 4-year degree after completing an associate degree in the technologies. If this is a goal, careful investigation of the possibilities is required because each situation seems to be different (this is not unique to technical education). The transferability of credits for degrees can be impossible, even between different branches of the same university. This situation has led legislators in some states to mandate transferability of college credits. In general, transferability of degrees or credits is most likely to occur in an ABET-approved program and least likely in a private career college.

Private Career Schools and Colleges of Technology

A major provider of pre-bachelor's degree postsecondary education is private career schools. In fact, about half of all postsecondary institutions are private or "proprietary" schools. These typically are small: 50% of institutions accredited by the Accrediting Commission of Career Schools and Colleges of Technology (ACCSCT) enroll 300 or fewer, and the average course lasts 47 weeks. National examples of such schools are ITT Education and Bryant Stratton (www.bryant-stratton.edu); others are regional, such as York Technical Institute in York, Pennsylvania (www.yti.edu). The relative importance of these schools in providing occupational preparation is not well known. For example, ITT graduates accounted for 11% of all electronics and electronics-related associate and bachelor's degrees awarded nationwide in 1994-95 and 19% of all degrees awarded in drafting. Private higher education was a $78 billion industry by the mid-1990s, 37% of all U.S. higher education expenditures. Private career colleges operate for profit, and they are typically more expensive than similar programs offered in publicly supported institutions such as community colleges. They survive, however, because they typically have very close ties with employers and have excellent placement services and placement rates. The programs are also often offered in a format geared to those who hold full-time jobs, and they are shorter in length because they do not require any nonrelated academic general studies courses.

Although the majority of private career colleges have been in existence for a long time and have excellent placement records, the industry has been plagued by some "here today, gone tomorrow" types. The accreditation organization recognized by the U.S. Department of Labor is the Accrediting Commission of Career Schools and Colleges of Technology (ACCSCT; www.accsct.org/). Only schools that are accredited and/or eligible to participate in financial student aid programs should be considered unless there are valid mitigating circumstances. If the goal is to acquire occupation-specific skills in a relatively short time and with a minimum of nonrelated academics, a maximum amount of hands-on experience, and a good chance of employment at the end, then private career colleges deserve a good look.

Distance Education

It is important to recognize a new alternative to higher education that began to develop in the late 1990s and has the potential to change radically the number of people who participate in higher education. By the late 1990s, almost every college and university was exploring ways to offer degrees via distance education, rather than on campuses, by using either Internet-based instruction or interactive video conferencing. Private colleges were the early leaders in this development. The University of Phoenix (www.vophx.edu), for example, offers both bachelor's and master's degrees and is accredited in all the states in which it operates. Currently, most distance education students are working adults; the University of Phoenix is thought to be the leading provider of higher education to working adults in the United States. And although the lure of campus life is unlikely to fade among teens in the near future, some would still prefer to stay at home. Now they can literally get a degree in their own living rooms.

Employer/Employee Provider Training

By any measure, employers are the largest provider and/or financier of post-high-school occupational training. According to a 1995 survey by the U.S. Department of Labor, 92% of employers provided, and 70% of employees received, formal employer-provided training; such instruction was planned in advance and had a structured format and a defined curriculum (Franzis, Gittleman, Horrigan, & Joyce, 1998). Thus, seeking employment that includes formal training tied to advancement on the career ladder is another alternative for graduating high school seniors. Formal training is more likely to be provided in mid-sized to large firms. Although formal training is more likely to be provided to older workers with some postsecondary education (Hight, 1998), the shortages of technical workers trained at the pre-bachelor's degree level that developed in the late

1990s led to increased interest among employers in recruiting and formally training graduating high school seniors, especially those who completed relevant vocational education programs. A graduating senior with a verified career interest and adequate math and science skills can find formal training opportunities in the all-important Craft/Precision Manufacturing/Specialized Repairs industries. Often, as part of this training, employers will finance an employee's part-time pursuit of an associate degree as well.

Formal Apprenticeship Programs

Perhaps the oldest model of occupational training is the formal apprenticeship. An apprenticeship differs from formal on-the-job training in several important ways. First, a state's department of labor typically regulates it; the curriculum and/or length of the experience, as well as the wage rates, are often mandated; and after the apprenticeship is completed, the result is a journeyman's license that may be used virtually anywhere in the world. Formal apprenticeship programs can be run by employers, by unions, or cooperatively by both through joint labor-management coordinating committees. Apprenticeship programs are typically found in the traditional construction and manufacturing crafts. Examples in the construction industry are boilermaker, bricklayer, carpenter, electrician, ironworker, painter, plasterer, plumber, and sheet metal worker. Some apprenticeship programs, such as those run by the plumbers and pipefitters locals, are very sophisticated, as well as competitive to get into. The program is 5 years in length and includes 1,080 hours of formal classroom instruction. Graduates emerge skilled in installation and maintenance of plumbing and heating, air-conditioning, or refrigeration units and may be trained as industrial controllers. On average, they will out-earn all college graduates except those who are successful in careers as managers or professionals. In fact, applicants for apprenticeship programs often already have college degrees. Information on apprenticeship programs that are available in a locale may be obtained by contacting the regional offices of the Bureau of Apprenticeship Training, a state's department of labor offices, employer or trade groups, or employers themselves. Although not all apprenticeship programs are registered with this state department, most of the better ones are.

High School Vocational Education

One alternative that is overlooked too often is a high school vo-
cational/technical education. Students who concentrate (take four
or more credits in the same vocational education program) in vocational education in high school and pursue a career in an occupation
that is the same or related to the one studied in high school will earn
16% to 35% more than those who take the college prep courses but
do not pursue a postsecondary education successfully (Gray &
Huang, 1993; Kang & Bishop, 1989). Vocational education graduates
are more likely not to drop out of high school and to be employed
after they graduate, which is important, considering that the youth
unemployment rate in the United States is typically double the overall unemployment rate. Just as important is the fact that high school
vocational education as a part of a two-plus-two (tech prep) program
can be a great way to move on to postsecondary pre-bachelor's degree technical education. The one very pragmatic reason for considering this option is, Why pay for a technical education that is equiva-
lent to a postsecondary certificate program when one can get the
same thing in high school for free?

Military Programs

The military is both a possible career choice and an opportunity
to obtain technical training. Although exact numbers are not available, there is little doubt that the military today is one source, if not
the leading source, of technicians. Importantly, and unlike in the
past, skills learned in military programs today are easily transferable
into civilian high-skill/high-wage careers. In fact, it is increasingly
common for an individual to serve her or his enlistment and then do
exactly the same type of work, often on the same type of equipment
and even at the same base, but employed by a private firm doing
contract work for the military. Also, unlike in the past, military programs today provide excellent opportunities for women, particularly in entry to high-skill/high-wage careers that are nontraditional
for them.

The military is also still a great place for some teens to grow up
and others to gain focus and confidence. Compared with some college campuses, it is a better, safer, and more inexpensive place to
develop maturity. Finally, military programs offer several financial

advantages. The training is free, and when the enlistment is over, help with tuition is available.

The Postgraduation, or "Prep," Year

For many teens, the relevant question should not be "What should I do after high school?" but rather "When should I do it?" Unfortunately, very few teens or parents are willing to address this question. Among the many attitudes that lead youths to almost certain failure after high school is the conventional "wisdom" that attending a 4-year college is not only the best thing to do after high school but must occur right after high school. Teens seem to worry that unless they go to college right away, their parents may not pay for it. Parents, in contrast, worry that unless their child goes to college right away, the child will not go later. Other, more subtle realities are also at work. Many parents' health plans will cover their children after high school only if they are in college. In addition, teens just don't seem to have enough things to do if they stay out of school for a year.

All these factors result in a general unwillingness to consider anything but college right away. It is interesting to observe that this development is a relatively recent one. In the 1960s and 1970s, it was relatively common for teens to take a "prep" year before continuing on. Often, this decision was a matter of necessity because students who were not qualified were not admitted. Open admissions and remedial education courses at most colleges changed the equation: Anyone who can fog a mirror can get in, so why take a prep year? How unfortunate. The reality is that many teens are just not ready for college. NAEP sources suggest that only about 40% are academically ready, and the solution—namely, college remediation—is largely ineffective with teens right out of high school. But even many students who are adequately prepared academically lack the commitment that comes from career maturity. Lacking this commitment, many of them, too, will fail. Finally, some students are just not emotionally ready to leave home and move into a dorm room with strangers. Add all of these together, and it is little wonder that the national college dropout rate is at historic highs.

Meanwhile, other data suggest that waiting a year is a predictor of success. According to one seemingly timeless finding from college persistence studies, older students do better. Readers can undoubtedly relate any number of personal, anecdotal stories about people who waited and succeeded or did not wait and failed but went back later and did well. Parents' fear that their children will not go to college at all if they wait a year are also groundless. My follow-up studies of recent high school graduates consistently show that teens who enter the labor force directly after high school most often indicate they are planning to attend an institution of higher education the following year.

How do colleges view taking a prep year, or a "gap" year, as it is referred to in Europe? To cite one statistic, about 2% of Princeton University's entering class has taken a prep year (Pereira, 1997). Often, students who take a year off have been admitted and then ask that their acceptance be deferred; most colleges agree to such requests.

Prep Year Options

The idea of taking a year off to prepare for postsecondary education, sometimes called a PG (postgraduation) or prep (preparation) year, is often not considered because of a lack of understanding of the reasons and options. Four reasons or objectives for taking a prep year are (a) academic preparation, (b) career exploration, (c) preparation to leave the nest, and (d) a need for something different.

Academic Preparation

For many teens, the reason for a prep or PG year is quite obvious after a look at their high school grades and college entrance exam scores. Perhaps as many as half are not ready. It makes little sense, however, to pay full tuition at a college to take remedial courses that do not count toward a degree and that are taught by part-time faculty or graduate students. More than that, it's simply a bad idea. There are better options.

The purpose of a PG year typically is to develop basic academic skills and thus improve college entrance exam scores. Undoubtedly, the best place to do a PG year is a school where the curriculum is designed for this purpose. A PG year is offered at many independent prep schools and typically involves a highly structured residential or boarding experience. Because college preparation is the sole mission and the faculty typically are well seasoned, such institutions offer an excellent opportunity. One example with a Web site is the Bridgton Academy in Bridgton, Maine (www.bacad.bridgton.me.us./banet/).

Although a residential PG year is expensive, it is no more so than a freshman year at a 4-year college. If the prognosis is that a student will be taking mostly remedial courses during the freshman year in college anyway, the cost of a PG year and the time to a degree will be about the same as matriculating right out of high school.

A less expensive alternative is to enroll as a nondegree candidate at a community college or even a 4-year college and take one or more academic courses. Because most institutions charge by the credit and because most allow nondegree students to take courses, enrolling in a few courses is less expensive than being a degree candidate. A word of caution needs to be added here, though: A PG year can be very effective in increasing academic skills but only if the student is motivated; a student who dislikes academics and lacks a good reason to go to college will probably not benefit from a PG year. A PG year is a good option, however, for teens who have academic talent but who woke up a little late to the importance of studying in high school. It is particularly good for teens who are chronologically or emotionally young, compared with others in their high school graduation class.

Career Exploration

Taking a year to develop a career focus is another wise choice for many teens. A few schools actually offer a high school postgraduation program designed especially for this purpose. Dynamy, in Worcester, Massachusetts, is one such institution offering an internship year (dynamy@nesc.org). The Dynamy experience consists of three different 9-week internships in areas such as law, wildlife management, photography, theater, publishing, and human services. Although most students continue on to college the next year, a few take the pre-bachelor's degree technical education route instead.

Students can, of course, develop their own 1-year internships while living at home. Sometimes people discover occupational preferences after they ascertain what they do not want to do for the rest of their lives; a year of hard knocks from working often leads to such conclusions. The goal for this year should be to develop and verify career interests. For example, working for a temp agency is one way to learn about a variety of firms and occupations and get paid for the opportunity. Finally, even though the goal is career focus, it is worth remembering that all jobs include formal and informal learning, which builds a teen's overall level of competence, including academic skills. A study done in the fast-food industry, for example, found that employed teens used 10 or more of the SCANS work skills daily on the job.

Preparation to Leave the Nest

For some students, a prep year is necessary just to get ready for the adjustment to life away from home. Taking a year off to work and take night courses while living at home and all their friends are away at college is an excellent way for some teens to grow up. Previous statistics regarding freshman dropout rates and the numbers who leave college in the first 3 weeks should be kept in mind. As is discussed in the next chapter, one of the greatest gifts parents can give their child is a willingness to see that college may be the right plan but that right after high school may not be the right time.

Need for Something Different

Some teens are emotionally troubled. Getting such teens to go to college is one thing; getting them to succeed is quite another, and the risk is high. College can be a very lonely place for some teens and thus a very dangerous place. College is also a very unstructured place: Students can elect not to go to class at all, and parents would not know whether their child went to class or not until they asked to see semester grades. Alternatives for such students include prep or developmental schools that cater to troubled youths. Some programs are therapeutic; others are designed simply to help students gain self-confidence and "grow up." One place to learn more about a sampling of such schools is the Woodbury Reports Web site (www.woodbury.com).

Promoting Success

It is amazing that, with the high cost of postsecondary education and the rising amount of student loan debt, few teens or parents even consider alternatives to a bachelor's degree. This reality alone begins to explain why so few are successful in college. A career-mature 18-year-old has verified a career or several related career choices. The usefulness of this focus is limited, however, if the student is unwilling to consider various postsecondary alternatives for developing the prerequisite skills necessary for labor market advantage in competing for opportunities. Thus, considering all the alternatives is the final ingredient in a postsecondary plan that has a high probability of success. All too often, the opposite seems to happen now: Students may have a fairly well thought-out career interest that calls for something other than a bachelor's degree education but enroll in a 4-year college anyway; most who do, fail. Taking these courses of action is both wasteful and expensive.

Among the many alternatives, taking a prep year needs to become acceptable if postsecondary success is the new priority. In the end, parents and the community are the most important influences on decisions like these; thus, in Chapter 7 the focus turns to parents and other adults who influence the decisions made by teens.

Talking to Parents and the Business Community

A better understanding of the relationship between career direction and postsecondary success has led high schools across the
nation to make instructional efforts that foster career maturity. Educators cannot do it alone. They must have the support of parents. As
long as parents are willing to tolerate, if not encourage, their children's fantasies about careers, career development efforts will have
little impact. Educators must also have the support of business and
industry, as well as community groups, to provide career develop-
ment/verification experiences. Messages designed to gain support
from each group are outlined in this chapter.

Talking to Parents

Clearly, academic skill is best developed when teachers and parents work together, with the latter's role to establish academic
achievement as a value. Efforts to develop career direction in teens
require the same support from home. In the end, what a student does
after high school is most often what parents at least tacitly approve.
More important, children will take career direction seriously when

their parents do. Thus, parents are crucial to the process, but they are also often a challenging group to reach and convince.

Parents are among the largest groups of believers in "one way to win" and perhaps even head the list. By the mid-1990s, over 80% of high school sophomores in a national study indicated that either their father or mother had recommended going to college (see Chapter 4, Table 4.5). And considering that 85% of the same group of students indicated planning to get a 4-year degree, it may be assumed that, to parents as well, college means a bachelor's degree-level education.

The extent of parental influence on post-high-school plans tends to be downplayed by teens themselves. Only 36% of entering freshmen in the study indicated, for example, that their "parents wanting them to go" was a very important reason for attending. Perhaps a better indicator is the extent of parents' contribution to the bill. Entering freshmen reported that parents were the most significant source of funds for college. Although a teen's friends may well wield the most influence when it comes to fashion, music, or entertainment, when it comes to what to do after high school, parents call the shots. Thus, although the extent of parental involvement varies, in the end most parents give at least tacit approval by writing a check.

For many parents, college is a source of worry and conflict. Findings from a 1997 American Council on Education (ACE, 1998) study revealed that college and college costs ranked only behind drug use as a source of parental concern. Importantly, the question where one's child will go to college has become the primary indicator of parental effectiveness in the United States. Many parents have heavy personal ego investments in this. For some, the success or failure of 12 years of parenting comes down to one thing—where their child goes to college. College means a bachelor's degree education. The reality is that those who would hope to improve postsecondary success for teens by improving career maturity and direction have two groups to convince: teens and their parents.

Timing Is Everything

Learning theory includes the concept of the "teachable moment," wherein instruction is effective when delivered at the time students are receptive (attentive). The same concept applies to parents. As their children proceed through school, parents in general become increasingly detached from the schools. Whereas parents' functions in the elementary schools draw large crowds, getting parents to high school gatherings is another story. Thus, a program that will effectively reach parents begins with the recognition of this reality.

Children's elementary years are the correct time to begin explaining to parents the concept of career maturity and the nexuses between career direction and postsecondary success. The best time to instill this value, at least in the long run, is at elementary school parents' functions, where this message may be repeated over and over again.

> Perhaps the most important predictor of the success of career development activities is the attitude that career and academic maturity are equally important. When parents believe this, progress will be made.

The junior high/middle school years, particularly those meetings with parents to discuss the transition to high school, may be the last of the major teachable moments that educators have to work with. Details regarding high school career development efforts, whether selection of academic courses or career major/pathways or the completion of an individual career plan, need to be presented to parents when they are listening—before their children get to high school. Parents need to be informed at this time about the school's expectations regarding parental involvement in these efforts.

Reaching parents of high school teens is difficult but not impossible if schools are willing to make the commitment to make it happen, especially by structuring situations requiring parental involvement and by making time during and after normal school hours to allow it to happen. For example, parent conferences could be made a prerequisite for course selection (see Chapter 5). Another effective method is to develop functions that address topics of parental concern, such as financial aid or college admissions.

Parents and Career Choice

Aside from generally believing the "one way to win" mantra and being under significant social pressure to send their children to a 4-year college, most parents share the national ambivalence about career planning, and ambivalence is the correct characterization. More often than not, parents hope their child's college graduation will mean commensurate employment, but at the same time they often are indifferent about the need for their teen to take career direction seriously. The reasons for this are many and complex. Some sense their child's confusion but do not know what to do about it, so they choose to ignore the issue. Some look at college as their last responsibility; what happens after it is not their problem. The majority, however, simply do not think that lack of career direction matters much because it was not a problem for them: When they were that age, it did not matter much.

Most parents of today's youths graduated from high school at a time when having a 4-year degree and breathing were the only prerequisites needed to pursue a career that ensured a place in the middle class. Twenty or more years ago, only one in seven who earned a BA degree were underemployed. Thus, many went to college with an "I'll see what happens when I graduate" attitude and still did OK. For this group, too, if college did not work out, high-wage jobs in manufacturing were a fallback. Now, many parents hold to the belief that the same will be true for their child. Of course, it will not. Interestingly enough, parents do seem to sense this. A parent whose child is an art history major or who belongs to the "major of the month" club is typically a worried parent. When polled, teens and parents both wish they had more opportunities to explore careers during the high school years. Thus, the problem is not so much a lack of parental receptiveness as a need to explain the importance of career maturity and career direction.

Parental Suspicions

Related to parental ambivalence about the importance of career choice is the outright suspicion among some parents that such efforts are really designed to keep their children from going to college. Parents who grew up in poverty, regardless of race and ethnicity, are prone to such suspicions, perhaps with good reason. For some parents, a college education—a 4-year college education—is seen as the only "hope" to escape poverty. Also, parents of children with troubled school histories, academic or otherwise, often blame the school system and therefore are likely to be suspicious as well. Others see career development activities within the schools or anywhere else as another indication of a trampling of families' rights.

Although these attitudes may seem a bit far-fetched, they are very real to those parents who hold them. Their suspicions are not based on a rejection of the need for career focus, however, but on their conception—rightly or wrongly—that the intent of such efforts is really to tell their children what they should or should not do. Thus, in their view, career development programs are really about persuading children. Therefore, it is crucial to involve parents in initial efforts to promote postsecondary success and then to maintain this involvement throughout their children's school years. With this and the other thoughts raised above in mind, let's look at a four-point format for talking to parents about planning for the postsecondary success for their children.

The plan is known as the "REAL" plan for postsecondary success. Its intent is to make parents and teens better decision makers and better consumers of higher education (if that is their hope and dream) and, of course, to improve teens' probability of postsecondary success.

A "REAL" Plan for Postsecondary Success

Remember the Goal:

BuyEr Beware

TAke Career Direction Seriously

Consider All ALternatives

The purpose of the REAL presentation to parents is to improve the probability of their children's postsecondary success. The plan includes four steps to effective postsecondary planning. The presentation begins with the assumption that all parents have college on their minds as a destination for their children. One objective is not to change their minds. Another objective is to broaden their perspectives regarding higher education, as well as other post-high-school alternatives. Although this presentation is designed for parents, it has proved to be as effective with teens.

Opening Remarks to Parents

When talking to parents, it is essential to assure them sometime in the first minutes that what their child does after high school is "their decision to make." Also, parents need to be assured that the presentation's intent is not to tell them what their child should or should not be doing, but rather to help them make the best decision possible and to be better consumers of higher education. To be more savvy consumers, they should know certain things, things they deserve to know. Thus, it is also useful to tell parents that the intent is not to trample on dreams, but to "tell it like it is." This is also a good time to make the point that although it is very possible to postpone dealing with the facts associated with going to college (e.g., career direction, academic skills, maturity) and that college itself makes it very easy to do so, in the end very few avoid these realities. It makes more sense to be "real" now than a year or two from now when the parents are paying tuition bills.

Step 1: Remember the Goal—Postsecondary Success

Like their children, most parents focus on college admissions rather than college success. As Dale Parnell pointed out in a 1998 address at a Virginia Tech Prep Conference, however, parents would be wise to focus on exit requirements, rather than on entrance requirements. Even though one may wish not to be so direct with parents, the reality is that overexpansions of higher education have made it possible for anyone to get into a 4-year college. To soften the message, simply report the numbers of college freshmen who come home for good in the first 3 weeks, take remedial courses, graduate, and so on. Most parents personally know one or more teens who are examples of these realities.

Perhaps the most effective way to get parents and teens to focus on the goal of success is to provide the type of labor market information contained in Chapters 2 and 3. This information is important in that it applies to both the academically talented and those from the academic middle. Regardless of credentials, most teens are in college for labor market advantage. The reality, however, is that commensurate employment will only be available for about half of those who actually earn 4-year degrees.

Reminding parents that the goal should be success, not college, seems to beg the question, "What does lead to success?" This is a good time to introduce the following point: Success for this generation will require academic skills, as well as a commitment to a career direction.

The bottom line is that the decision is theirs and their child's to make but that some plans have a higher probability of success than others. Plans that lead to success are the result of considering the remaining three steps.

Step 2: Buyer Beware

A key to successful postsecondary planning is to view it both as an educational decision and as a costly expenditure. Parents should try to approach it in the same way they would if they were spending at least $40,000 on something else—a little healthy skepticism is called for. When getting ready to make any purchase of this magnitude, it is wise to recall the advice *caveat emptor,* or buyer beware. Colleges, for example, never discuss costs; they only discuss financial aid. What they do not reveal is that financial aid is now just a code word for debt (see Figure 7.1).

Whereas in the 1970s, less than half of a financial aid package was loans, today's packages are about two thirds loans. Higher education is a buyer's market—not at the 200 or so medallion colleges and universities where admissions are very competitive, but almost everywhere else. Like any buyer's market, consumers are advised to be skeptical or at least cautious. Much information about colleges is misleading. Perhaps the best indicator of this point is the fact that federal higher education legislation now requires higher education institutions to supply students with "right to know" information, including graduation rates. Congress would not require this if it were not needed. Although the implication here is not that colleges necessarily lie to students, they do tend to be very selective about the information they supply. An interesting question, for example, concerns the number of faculty really on the faculty, not adjunct or part-time.

Another example of the need for caution is remedial or developmental courses. Most parents are clueless about remedial education

Figure 7.1. Carrying more debt: Loans make up a larger percentage of college costs.

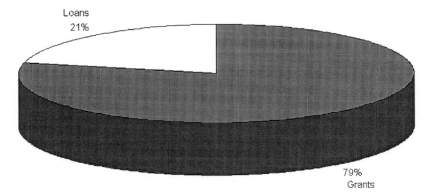

Figure 7.1a. 1974-1975 In Constant 1994 Dollars (millions)
Total: 24,371

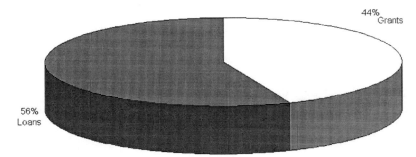

Figure 7.1b. 1994-1995 In Constant 1994 Dollars (millions)
Total: 46,167
SOURCE: NCES #98-076 (1996).

in college. They deserve to know that colleges admit students who cannot do academic work at that level before actually determining whether these potential freshmen have the skills to do college-level work. Most colleges require those admitted to take placement tests whose results lead to either required or strongly recommended enrollment in remedial or makeup courses that do not count toward a degree. Parents should also be told that remedial education may be a second chance for some teens, but for most teens right out of high school it predicts the strong potential not to graduate from college. They also should be reminded that such courses increase both the cost of the degree and the time it takes to finish. In addition, it is useful to tell parents that the average university student at a public institution now takes more than 5 years to finish.

The Wisdom of a Backup Plan

Perhaps the most important piece of specific advice associated with Step 2 is to have a backup plan: a Plan A and a fallback Plan B. For most parents and teens, Plan A will be the "one way to win" plan. When considering Plan B, however, they should be considering all alternatives (Step 4). Of course, having a Plan B is of little value to planners who are unwilling to consider anything but Plan A. Knowing when and having the courage to consider Plan B is the essence of Step 4. If more parents were willing to be objective, willing to have a backup plan, and willing to recognize when Plan B should become Plan A, more students would enjoy post-high-school success.

Step 3: Take Career Direction Seriously

The third step of the REAL plan for postsecondary success is to recognize the importance of having career direction as a basis for making postsecondary plans that lead to success. Whereas most parents' hopes and dreams for their child include college and a job afterward, few take career focus seriously. The objective of Step 3 is to challenge this point of view.

Step 3 stems from the reality that commitment is as important as academic skills in predicting postsecondary success. This is not a matter of opinion, but rather is based on research findings that have consistently shown that uncertainty about academic majors and career goals is linked to failure. Cope and Hannah (1975) found in a national study that commitment to a career goal and thus to an educational goal is the most important factor determining persistence to graduate.

The point about the importance of career focus to parents is perhaps best made by reminding them that most teens drop out of college in the sophomore year, when a college academic major must be selected. Although they may believe/hope that their child will develop career focus in college, in most cases this thinking is wishful. The reality is that college is a terrible place to try to sort out career interests. Developing career focus requires exposure to reality, and few institutions are more detached from reality than colleges and universities. In fact, some people become professional students to avoid the reality of the outside world. Not only is college a bad place to develop career direction, but it is also a very expensive place to do so. Success stems from going to college or engaging in any other post-high-school pursuit, committed to finding an answer to the question "Why college?" For most, answering why includes beginning a career after completing a degree.

Another good way to emphasize the importance of career direction is to show parents some supply-and-demand figures for typical occupations (see Chapters 2 and 3) to demonstrate that more people will be in line who have degrees than commensurate employment is available. Most parents are sobered by the fact that only 57 jobs requiring a 4-year degree are available for every 100 recipients. At this point, one may wish to challenge the conventional wisdom about career decisions closing doors. Keep in mind that this generation does not have to worry about closing doors: All doors to high-skill/high-wage work are already closed because either there are too many people for the number of openings or the skill set is specific to an elite group of people. Most parents do not acknowledge this reality, nor is it what they have been led to believe.

Citing the variables that will determine which college graduates will receive commensurate employment also emphasizes for parents the importance of career direction. Remember that today even those who graduate from college with good grades end up underemployed. Labor market competitive advantage comes from skills, not degrees. The final point to make is obvious: If the key to high-skill/high-wage work is having skills that are in demand, then a prerequisite decision involves determining the career in which to develop skills. The ability to make career decisions becomes the basis for making postsecondary plans that result in relevant skills. The sooner teens gain this ability, the longer they will have to develop these skills and the sooner they will get in line.

Even though many parents indicate some understanding of the importance of career direction, they do not know how to help their children with it. In times past, parents tended to encourage their children to follow in their footsteps. This is no longer the case. When polled, a majority of parents would not recommend having their children pursue the same career as they did, and most teens, when polled, seem to agree: The agreement here highlights the need for school-based and community-support career development programs for youths.

It is useful to tell parents exactly what the outcome goal for their child should be. Parents of young children often jump to the conclusion that the goal is to force decisions at a very early age, but that's not true. By the end of the 10th grade, however, children should be able to identify several career interests that can be verified in the 11th and 12th grades. The results of this verification should become the most important aspect of a postsecondary plan based strongly on well-researched and thought-out occupational motives. The next step is to consider "all" the alternatives to achieving the desired career goal.

Step 4: Consider All the Alternatives

The final step in the REAL plan for postsecondary success is to consider all the alternatives. The four listed here are condensed from those discussed in Chapter 6.

- 4-year bachelor's degree education
- Postsecondary technical education
- Military/Formal apprenticeships
- The PG or prep year

In the formal presentation to parents, little time is spent discussing the 4-year alternative except the reality that objective student achievement data suggest (a) it is a good alternative for about 40% of all high school graduates, (b) only about half ever graduate, and (c) of those who do, only about half will find commensurate employment.

Conversely, considerable time is spent discussing the postsecondary technical education alternatives and high-skill/high-wage nonprofessional employment (see Chapter 6). It is useful to have one or more lists to demonstrate exactly the occupations being referred to. Such lists are particularly useful in pointing out the diversity of careers. Research indicates that although future earnings are important to youths, what they really hope is to find a career that will provide sufficient earnings and some happiness. Thus, stressing the diversity of work environments is important, as is contrasting the opportunities in these occupations with the hordes competing for post-bachelor's degree employment. It is also important to mention that, in many cases, 2-year degrees are transferable to 4-year degree programs and that often employers will pay for the last 2 years.

Perhaps the most important option to present to parents is the one that everyone seems to have forgotten but that, for many teens, is the very best choice—namely, taking a year off to find some career direction and/or get better academically prepared (see Chapter 6). Often, it makes much more sense for a student with poor academic credentials to work full-time and take one or two college remedial courses as a part-time student than to pay full tuition as a full-time student taking only developmental courses.

A consideration of all the alternatives implies that a decision must be made. Thus, the presentation of the REAL plan for postsecondary success should conclude with a discussion of the clues provided by teens regarding what they are really ready to do after high school. The clues are called *wake-up calls.*

Listening for Wake-Up Calls

The final step in the REAL plan for postsecondary success is to consider all the post-high-school options. But how will a parent know the best option or when Plan B should become Plan A? One way to address this touchy question is to urge parents to listen to wake-up calls.

Many parents send their child to certain failure in college. Why? Because they simply are unwilling or fail to hear the wake-up calls signaling that college attendance may not be a good idea for their child. But how does one recognize a wake-up call? The following list was provided by a group of undergraduate college students:

Wake-Up Calls

(Or how parents can know when college is not a good idea, at least not now.)

Obvious Wake-Up Calls

Having poor high school grades

Having poor college admission test scores

Lacking a career direction ("I don't know what I want to do")

Feeling that school has always been a source of conflict ("I hate school")

Not liking to read

Always requiring close parental supervision to complete school-work

Frequently cutting high school classes

Not graduating with their class

Having trouble with the law; trouble with drugs

Not So Obvious Wake-Up Calls

Being evasive about postsecondary plans (doesn't want to talk about it)

Having "How much work do I have to do?" as their only academic interest

Avoiding taking the college entrance test (SAT, ACT)

Never getting around to filling out college application

Not applying to a college that requires an essay

Having parents filling out applications and writing the essays

Applying only to the school where their boyfriends or girl-friends are going

Showing no interest in visiting college campuses

Passively letting parents decide where to apply

Delaying until the last possible moment to prepare to leave for college

Applying to colleges on the basis of difficulty of the application, where friends are going, nice climate, good skiing, and so on

Parents themselves, especially those with children already in college, probably could add to these lists. Although some groups consider it humorous, it is not funny to all. The wake-up calls are often conscious acts by teens to send a message they hope will be heard. Of course, teens often ignore their own wake-up calls. "Getting real" means hearing them.

Helping Parents With Difficult Choices

When working with parents, and teens as well, it is important to realize that postsecondary planning is a very emotional issue. Planning their child's post-high-school direction is not easy for most parents, particularly those whose children are in the academic middle. Many dinners have been ruined by discussions about such questions as "What exactly are you going to do next year?" or statements like "I think you should . . ." Future plans are not easy conversation topics in many homes and thus need to be addressed with an appropriate level of understanding and compassion.

How can parents and teens work most effectively to promote postsecondary success? Way and Rossman (1996), among others, have found that families typically take one of three approaches: (a) "I know best," (b) "Hands off," and (c) "Let's discuss it." Only one of the three is really effective in promoting postsecondary success.

The approach "I know best; do as I say" is typical of domineering parents. This approach is very effective in getting teens to go to 4-year colleges. Research suggests that it is very ineffective in getting them to graduate. Importantly, in the "I know best" approach, the responsibility for decisions is with the parent, not the teen. Remember that commitment is a prime predictor of postsecondary success; these teens are not committed.

The equally common approach "hands off" is the opposite of the "I know best" approach. Many parents seem worn out by 12 years of parenting. Rather than face more conflict with their child, they take a passive approach and just let whatever happens happen and then pay for it later. Many parents view their child's college education as their last financial responsibility and limit their involvement accordingly. What happens thereafter is not their responsibility. This approach, too, is not very effective. Often, good students who should be in 4-year colleges do not go, and vice versa. More important, lacking emotional support from home, these teens often fold under the pressures of college academics and college life.

The most effective approach is the democratic, or "Let's discuss it," approach. The topic of life after high school is discussed openly and early. Parents set parameters early. One example is the message

"I will support you in college to the extent possible but only when you are ready for college," which sets a useful parameter. In this case, *ready* means maturity, which includes career maturity. Perhaps most important, parents are willing to listen to the messages or wake-up calls their children send them in a thousand different little ways. Whereas parents who take either the "I know best" or the "hands off" approach ignore or miss these messages, wise parents listen, hear the wake-up calls, and act accordingly. Alas, this is easier said than done. Making this point is often a good way to end discussions on career maturity with parents.

Talking to the Business Community

Developing career maturity and career direction is best accomplished by providing opportunities to verify tentative interests via exposure to real workplaces and workers. Thus, efforts to help teens "get real" will not be successful without the involvement of the business community. The challenge is to get businesses to look beyond the immediate need to find skilled workers and realize that their problem is rooted in the misguided decisions made by teens and parents. Thus, while employers face immediate labor shortages, the long-run solution depends on teens and their parents making better decisions in the future. Getting the business community involved in career maturity/career direction efforts typically begins with getting employers to realize this point. Many national trade organizations have come to this conclusion, so making this point is not as difficult as it may seem. The following rationale can be used when talking to the business community.

Skills Shortages and Today's Youths: What's Really Going On?

Even the most casual observer of the U.S. economic scene would conclude that the mismatch between the labor force needs of national firms and the skills of the country's citizens is colossal. One often-heard hypothesis on this dilemma is that the nation's schools are not providing workers with the skills that industry needs. It is valid to suggest that, at least when it comes to recent high school graduates, this type of thinking is shortsighted; but, in fact, it misses the point altogether.

The problem is not a skills mismatch caused by schools, but a mismatch between the hopes and dreams of today's youths and what firms need. Firms need individuals with technical skills, but many teenagers want to be doctors, lawyers, or engineers.

Today's teens and their parents have wrongly concluded that there is only "one way to win" left in America—namely, get a 4-year college degree. Why? To ensure a good job. Where? In the professional occupations.

In a national study of 1992 high school graduates (NCES, 1992), 95% indicated planning to seek further education, whereas 85% indicated aspirations toward at least a 4-year college degree. When asked about the type of job they hoped to have when they reached age 30, 49% of all youths in this study and an amazing 69% of all young women in the study indicated a desire to be employed in various occupations classified as Professional. Less than 5% of all youths surveyed indicated an interest in Technical or Craft/Precision Manufacturing/Specialized Repair occupations, all of which are areas of critical labor shortages and high wages.

The problem starts to come into focus when one considers that, according to the latest U.S. Department of Labor forecasts (Silvestri, 1997), only 23% of all employment in the next 10 years will require a 4-year college degree or higher. It would be a mistake to dismiss the aspirations of today's youths as quixotic wishful thinking. Immature, yes, unrealistic, certainly, but not wishful. Why? Because most youths attempt to pursue this dream, albeit at great expense and— for most—with little success.

College attendance by graduating high school seniors is at historic levels. Less than one third of all youths do anything but go to college directly after high school. Those who do go directly to work—only around 23%—are, on average, from the lowest high school academic quartiles.

Thus, it is not surprising that the nation's firms cannot find young workers with the level of ability they need; all but 17% of them are in 4-year colleges or in general studies transfer programs at 2-year institutions.

The folly of this "one way to win" mentality lies in its harmful effects on youths and their parents. Going to college is not a benign proposition. Less than half (40%) of all youths who graduate from high school are prepared to do college-level academics. Another 30% who go to college anyway end up in remedial catch-up courses. At best, only about half graduate 6 years later. But more than half have one thing in common: They borrowed money to pay tuition. In fact, it has been suggested that, for many, college results in a "mortgage minus the house" whether they graduate or not.

Of those who do graduate, many end up disappointed. Among graduates with degrees in professional areas (e.g., engineering, teaching, accounting), only one in two finds commensurate employment. What do those who cannot find college-level work do? Many become reverse transfers, enrolling in 1- and 2-year technology programs to learn job skills. Others go to graduate school and still end up underemployed. It makes no sense.

What do we do about it? More specifically, What can the leading firms in the nation do about it? Criticizing the public schools for the shortage of skilled workers will do little, if any, good. Instead, it would be more effective to focus on helping youths and their parents, many of whom are their employees, make better—more realistic—decisions.

Employer's Role

What is the appropriate role for business and industry in helping students and parents make more informed postsecondary choices? First and foremost, the goal is not to talk parents into or out of anything. This should be clear from the beginning, lest the public view corporate efforts as self-serving.

Post-high-school plans are the purview of each teenager and his or her parents. The goal is to help them become more informed consumers of higher education and thus make more realistic decisions. For teens, the first ingredient of being an informed consumer is an appropriate level of career maturity. This means being able to make tentative decisions about career aspirations that can serve as a focus or foundation for postsecondary planning. National firms can play a major role in fostering career maturity among today's teens. Here are five things firms can do:

1. Focus the community on success of students, not on the number of students sent to college. The reality is that most of the nation's schools and colleges take the majority of those who apply. College admission has few barriers, including ability to do college-level academics. Community recognition of firms' concerns with results puts

these firms in a unique position to suggest the need to move toward recognition of postsecondary success and to remind the community that success depends as much on career focus as on academic skills.

2. Be specific about the opportunities in your industry and what skills and/or credentials are required. All too often, industry is too vague; the vacuum caused by this lack of specificity can lead to the wrong conclusions about the need for a 4-year degree. A classic case in point is media attention on "information technology" (IT) workers. Predictably, the nation's colleges will use this emerging job market to persuade youths to get a 4-year edge. In reality, however, fewer than 20% of the occupations in this area will require a 4-year degree.

3. Stress the importance of skills in hiring decisions. Teenagers think that all they need is a degree in any area. If the type and area of the degree do matter, start saying so publicly. If you are looking at both degrees and evidence of ability to apply knowledge (skills) in your core business, say so. If, in your industry, skills certificates are more important than degrees, say so.

4. Support technical education if you really need technicians. Most firms in the nation can hire twice as many engineers and MBAs as they need. Yet, they continue to focus most of their support on graduates from 4-year colleges. Why? Technical education, both secondary and postsecondary, is in jeopardy in the United States, withering on the vine from a lack of funds and students. It needs your support. For most firms in this country, the fate of postsecondary technical education is much more important to long-term competitiveness than are the nation's 4-year colleges.

5. Support school-to-work and other public school efforts to expose teenagers to the world of work, such as career pathways and tech prep. The public school system is beginning to recognize the importance of helping youths attain a level of career maturity. They cannot succeed, however, without access to the world of work. They need your help. Become an advocate for their efforts.

Many of today's teenagers are seriously adrift. In all too many cases, their hopes and dreams are seriously out of sync with reality.

As a result, U.S. industry experiences labor shortages in key areas and must recruit technicians from abroad. This problem should not be blamed on teenagers who, in many cases, are clueless because they have few clues except the constant drumming of the message "Go to college." In the long run, getting the workforce that industry needs depends on more informed decisions from today's youths and their parents. A 4-year college degree is the right plan for some, but not all, teenagers; until this reality sinks in, skills shortages will persist. Industry has a role, perhaps the major role, to play in countering the "one way to win" mentality.

Ways Business Can Help With Youth Career Development

Few from the business community are willing to commit to being involved in youth career development efforts until they know exactly what they are being asked to do. The following list, based on the employer participation model of the National Employer Leadership Council, is effective in communicating a variety of roles.

Career Awareness/Career Verification

- Internships
- Job shadowing
- Industry tours
- Career seminars

Career Preparation

- Cooperative education
- Apprenticeships
- Formal on-the-job training
- Mentoring

Working with Educators

- Subject matter experts for curriculum/instructional development
- Participation in information programs for parents

Community Leadership

- Local advocates for career development efforts
- State advocates for career development efforts

Promoting Success

Efforts to promote postsecondry success by developing career maturity/career direction require, at a minimum, the support of parents and the business community. Addressing these groups was the topic of this chapter. The REAL plan for postsecondary success was suggested as a format for presentations to parents. An approach for addressing the business community was also provided. The key to both is to make sure the audience understands that the goal is helping teens and parents make better decisions, not making the decisions for them. In the end, the current quiet dilemma in which good jobs go vacant and college graduates are filling out applications at the mall will not improve until everyone involved is willing to stop delivering "nutritional lies" (Kramer, 1998) to today's youths and to help them "get real" instead.

```
┌─────────────────────┐
│ ║  Chapter 8  ║ │
└─────────────────────┘
```

Nutritional Lies
or Reality?

American youths grow up being fed a steady diet of "nutritional lies" (Kramer, 1998), pearls of wisdom fed to children that are false but thought to be healthy—thus nutritional—for them to believe. The "one way to win" mantra—that getting a 4-year degree will ensure financial success later in life—is a nutritional lie. Another is the assurance given to confused and unfocused teens that all will become clear in college. Still another is "You'd better go to college right after high school or else you never will." Nutritional lies are fine if the benchmark is maximizing postsecondary enrollments, but they are counterproductive if the benchmark is postsecondary success.

The intent of nutritional lies—namely, to encourage children to be ambitious—is noble. Often, the result is not. For most who swallow such lies, things never fall into place. College life leaves many even more confused and unfocused; only about half graduate in 6 years, and of those who do, only about half find employment commensurate with their level of education.

Thus, in the end, nutritional lies often turn out to be downright unhealthy. And in the end, when teens discover as young adults that they have been fed lies, they feel betrayed, and they have every right to feel that way. Talk to a recent bachelor's degree graduate who is living at home and working at the mall! She or he was told, "Just get a degree and everything will work out," and of course, for many, it doesn't.

Although nutritional lies may be benign for children, for adolescents they become toxic. By the 10th grade, such lies serve only as opiates, protecting teens from the pain of "getting real." Unfortunately, the narcotic effect of nutritional lies is limited. In the end, avoiding reality can have costly and personally painful consequences, with the pain shared by both the teens and their parents. As children approach their teenage years, they are best served by adults helping them gain a grip on reality, not feeding them lies. Even though most adults accept the logic of this approach, they often are unwilling to get teens to face realities or are ambivalent about it. They worry that "reality" will discourage teens and thus possibly limit their opportunity.

Creating Opportunity

At the heart of the "get real" point of view is a different philosophy on the best ways to provide opportunity for all teens. Instead of nutritional lies, it argues that success—thus opportunity—is maximized when teens are helped to develop postsecondary goals and plans based on the realities they will face as young adults. This issue has been a consistent dilemma for Americans. Whereas the culture encourages aspirations, its economic system is notoriously stingy at producing universal opportunity. The problem, again, is that "getting real" means facing this reality, and many adults are unwilling to deliver the news.

As argued more than 30 years ago by eminent sociologist Burton Clark (1962), the nation has opted for what he terms the "ideology of equal opportunity." Adults go to great lengths to shield youths from reality, to provide unlimited access to higher education, and by so doing they cleverly make the nation's colleges and labor market deliver the Darwinian news. Ultimately, the fit survive while the less fit fail. In the now infamous article "The 'Cooling Out' Function in Higher Education," Clark observes that the nation has chosen a "soft response" to limited opportunity, spending billions to expand higher education and thereby virtually assuring anyone who can fog a mirror an opportunity to try. Satisfied that it has done what it can, it turns a blind eye as the higher education system and the labor market deliver harsh reality to youths. Of course, this all works best if youths are fed a steady diet of nutritional lies in the meantime.

Those who adhere to what could be termed the "get real" school of thought reject nutritional lies and find the high failure rates associated with higher education/labor market Darwinism unacceptable. Absolutely no evidence supports the notion that justice is served by delivering nutritional lies that lead the nation's youths to failure with mathematical certainty. Hopes and dreams based on fantasy are just that—fantasy—but not a benign fantasy. It is costly and malignant. Rather than creating opportunity, it leads to failure.

Helping youths temper their postsecondary goals with reality is not stepping on their dreams, but rather is cultivating the probability of future success. Serving nutritional lies, in contrast, is ensuring that reality will crush the hopes and dreams of many teens. Encouraging teens to pursue goals that are difficult but doable is responsible. Encouraging youths to ignore reality and set totally undoable goals or to avoid goals altogether is irresponsible; doing so leads, in the vast majority of cases, to frustration, failure, and most important, lack of confidence to develop and pursue future career goals.

To summarize, if the goal is just getting as many teens into 4-year colleges as possible and not worrying about what happens thereafter, nutritional lies are fine. But if the goal is postsecondary success, then nutritional lies are counterproductive. The goal argued in this book is postsecondary success. All youths should be helped to develop difficult but doable goals. Toward this end, the following five premises are offered.

Five Premises for Success

This book argues five premises in support of the need to help teens "get real." These are reviewed below.

Premise 1: It's time to stop counting how many teens go to college and start counting how many do so successfully.

The first premise is based on the assertion that it is time for schools and the nation to move beyond the obsession with ascertaining the percentage of youths who go to college. At one time, such a benchmark may have had meaning, but it is long past in most communities—not in all perhaps, but in most. In today's environment of higher education overexpansion and remedial education, college attendance is a meaningless measure of a school system's effectiveness; for the vast majority of today's youths, all barriers to college have been removed, including the ability to do college-level academics. It is time to move on to ask a more fundamental question: How many graduates are successful, particularly in that important first or second year after high school?

> Premise 2: Every student should graduate from high school with a postsecondary plan that has a high probability of success.

The second premise of this book is that if the goal of teens is success, then the appropriate outcome for graduating high school students is a developed and implementable postsecondary plan that has a high probability of success. This goal is quite different from that which gets as many teens as possible to enroll in higher education. Planning assumes purposefulness or a desired end. College is not an end, but a means to an end. Although most teens will say that the intent is to get a better job in the future, few struggle with the details. For many teens, going to college is the default plan; college has become a place to avoid having to "get real." Developing an effective postsecondary plan requires the skills associated with career maturity, including an understanding of the importance of planning for success and the importance of being objective or honest about one's aptitudes, skills, likes, and dislikes.

> Premise 3: Postsecondary success depends on both academic skills and commitment, which come from career maturity and direction.

The third premise is that the cornerstone of postsecondary is now the commitment that comes from career maturity and career direction more than from academic skills. The overexpansion of higher education has made it all but impossible to flunk out of most colleges; thus, lack of commitment is now the main reason for dropping out of college. In fact, the main reason students leave college is that they have no reason to stay. If they had a goal or a career direction or both, more would stay. In fact, those who have a direction are more likely both to graduate and to find commensurate employment.

Premise 4: By the 10th grade, teens should have moved from fantasy to identifying tentative career interests. In the 11th and 12th grades, schools should help teens verify these interests and use these experiences as a basis for formulating postsecondary plans.

The fourth premise concerns instructional objectives for career development efforts. Often, such efforts fail because of a lack of specific goals.

Two very specific goals have been argued in this book. The first goal for career development efforts in the elementary and middle school years is to assist students in making "tentative" career choices by the 10th grade. In some cases, students may have several tentative career choices, which is fine if the choices are related either by skills required or work performed. The second goal for career development efforts is to assist high school juniors and seniors in verifying tentative career interests. It is important that this developmental stage be reached by the 10th grade for two reasons. First, it allows a student 2 more years in high school to take the courses and develop the prerequisite skills/credentials to implement a relevant postsecondary plan. Second, it allows a student time to verify these tentative choices while in high school, not later while paying college tuition. The importance of this verification cannot be overstated. Even among those students who go off to college in demanding majors, such as engineering or health care, many have no idea what they are getting into, and when they find out, they do not like it. This is just as true for the academically blessed as for those in the academic middle.

The final premise of this book is that developing postsecondary plans is predicated on a willingness to consider all the alternatives.

> Premise 5: A REAL plan for postsecondary success includes considering all the alternatives.

This requires, for example, special efforts to ensure that career options considered by teens are not narrowed by gender, race, or other stereotypes. This also requires a consideration of all types of high-skill/high-wage employment, not just that necessary for a professional career.

A REAL postsecondary plan includes a willingness to consider all available options for career preparation beyond a 4-year college degree. For example, 2-year postsecondary technical education is an excellent alternative; it is less expensive than bachelor's degree education, and most fields for which students are trained have labor shortages. The military and apprenticeship programs are also excellent opportunities. Finally, some youths need to consider taking a year to get ready. Some call it a prep year (in Europe, it's called a "gap" year), and it is taken to spend a year growing up, improving academic skills, and/or developing a career focus. Remember that students who take this route do better, as a group, than those who go to college right after high school.

Well-Intended But Bad
Advice Given to Teens

The five premises for teenage postsecondary success contradict several pieces of conventional advice. These are reviewed here to show that although they may still dominate, they are no longer valid.

The first piece of conventional advice is that career decisions should be postponed as long as possible because, once made, they somehow limit opportunities or "close doors." The implication of this advice is that all doors to careers are open. This has always been a nutritional lie, of course, but it was less so 30 years ago, when only 40% of youths went on to higher education and only about 20% of all youths finished. In those days, individuals who did persist were in high demand, many doors were open, and graduates had many options. Today, the situation has reversed: All doors are closed either because there are too many applicants for every opportunity or because the skill level is so specific that only those with such skills are hired. For this generation, a university degree is just a ticket to get in line, and the line is to an oversold event. Getting in requires a special ticket called an occupational skill. Developing such skills requires a prerequisite decision about the type of career in which to develop skills. Those who postpone such decisions will be the last in line and more than likely will never get in.

The second piece of well-meaning but nevertheless insidious advice is that lack of career direction is nothing to worry about—that teens "can decide that in college." The problem is that, for many, lightning never strikes. College is a very bad place to be trying to develop career direction. Making such decisions requires contact with the real world, and few places are more detached from reality than universities. Colleges are great places to avoid reality, and many students are there for that very reason. Thus, to suggest that college life will lead to career direction and eventually to commitment is a nutritional lie.

Understanding Our Role

A discussion of the five premises for teenage postsecondary success should include a reiteration of the role of educators, business and industry, and the community in general in this developmental process. Much of the ambivalence about career development activities for teens can be traced to a lack of clarity on this issue. Too often, it is thought that the purpose of career development programs is to tell teens—and their parents—what they should or should not do after high school. This misconception leads to much ambivalence among educators and suspicion of such efforts by some parents.

Decisions about postsecondary plans should only be made by the teens and their parents. School- or community-sponsored career development efforts should not alter this reality in any way. The objective is to help teens and parents make better decisions, be better consumers of higher education, and increase the odds of success. An individual maximizes her or his human potential by becoming aware of all options and by being willing to deal with the realities of life. The goal is not to tell some teens that they should not go to college, but to ensure that they are aware of all alternatives.

Fighting the Good Fight

The goals argued in this book will not come easily. It has taken 40 years to get to this point. Many parents and members of the public at large do not grasp the fact that the labor market realities faced by this generation are not the ones they themselves faced. Unhappily, and in addition, serving nutritional lies has become the norm. Yet, it is important to remember that, when polled, both parents and students indicated a desire for more opportunities to explore careers in the public school years.

Nevertheless, the work is frustrating and requires patience. Often in America, "the good is held hostage to the perfect," meaning that small gains are discounted because total success is not achieved. Those who seek to improve postsecondary success by helping youths "get real" should keep this in mind. If every effort and activity reach at least one teen, progress has been made and the effort has been worthwhile. Helping teens "get real" is the tonic to nutritional lies. We fight the good fight!

References

American Council on Education (ACE). (1998). *The American freshman national norms for fall 1997*. Washington, DC: Author.

American Vocational Education Association. (1997). *Mid-Atlantic guide to information on careers*. Washington, DC: Author.

Astin, A. W., & Dey, E. L. (1989). *Predicting college student retention: Comparative national data from the 1982 freshman class*. Berkeley: University of California, Higher Education Research Institute.

Bean, J. P., & Metzner, B. S. (1996). *Retention-attrition in the 90s*. Washington, DC: Office of Educational Research and Improvement. (ERIC Document Reproduction Service No. ED 393-510)

Bianchi, J. (1998). *An analysis of variables influencing eighth-grade students' career awareness*. Unpublished doctoral dissertation, Penn State University, University Park.

Bishop, J. (1995). *Expertise and excellence*. Ithaca, NY: Cornell University, Center for Advanced Human Resource Studies.

Callan, P. (1998, March). *Concept paper*. Washington, DC: National Center for Public Policy and Higher Education.

Campbell, C., & Dahir, C. (1997). *The national standards for school counseling programs*. Alexandria, VA: American School Counselors Association.

Carey, A., & Parker, S. (1998, February 27). Class of 01 not their parents. *USA Today*.

Clark, B. (1962). The "cooling out" function in higher education. *American Journal of Sociology, 65*, 576-596.

Cope, R., & Hannah, W. (1975). *Revolving open doors.* New York: John Wiley.

Cunanan, E., & Maddy-Bernstein, C. (1997, October). *1996 national exemplary career guidance programs: Making the connection.* Macomb: Western Illinois University, National Center for Research in Vocational Education.

Eccles, J. (1994). Understanding women's educational and occupational choices. *Psychology of Women Quarterly, 18,* 585-609.

Educational Testing Service (ETS). (1989). *High-achieving Hispanic students* (ETS Policy Notes, V1, 1-3). Princeton, NJ: Author. (ERIC Document Reproduction Service No. 338 632)

Farmer, H. (1995). *Gender differences in adolescent career exploration.* (ERIC Document Reproduction Service No. ED 391 108)

Fisher, T., & Griggs, M. (1995). Factors that influence the development of African American and Latino youth. *Journal of Vocational Education Research, 20*(2), 57-73.

Franzis, H., Gittleman, M., Horrigan, M., & Joyce, M. (1998, June). Results from the 1995 survey of employer-provided training. *Monthly Labor Review,* 3-13.

Gray, K., & Herr, E. (1995). *Other ways to win: Creating alternatives for high school graduates.* Thousand Oaks, CA: Corwin.

Gray, K., & Herr, E. (1996, May 6). BA degrees should not be "the only way." *Chronicle of Higher Education,* p. B1.

Gray, K., & Huang, N. (1991). Quantity or quality: An analysis of the impact of increased graduation requirements on math and science courses completed by vocational education graduates in Pennsylvania. *Journal of Vocational Education Research, 16*(1), 37-51.

Gray, K., Huang, N., & Li, J. (1993). The gender gap and yearly earnings: Is it a lack of education or occupational segregation? *Journal of Vocational Education Research, 18*(3), 1-14.

Herr, E., & Cramer, S. (1996). *Career guidance through the life span* (5th ed.). New York: HarperCollins.

Hight, J. (1998, June). Young worker participation in post-school education and training. *Monthly Labor Review,* 14-21.

Holland, J. (1994). *Self-directed search.* Odessa, FL: Psychological Assessment Resources.

Information Technology Association of America (ITA). (1998). *Help wanted: A call for collaborative action for the new millennium.* Blacksburg: Virginia Polytechnic Institute.

Joyner, C. (1998, March 27). *Information technology* (HEHS-98-106R). Washington, DC: General Accounting Office.

Judy, R., & D'Amico, C. (1997). *Workforce 2020: Work and workers in the 21st century.* Indianapolis, IN: Hudson Institute.

Kang, S., & Bishop, J. (1989). Vocational and academic education in high school: Complements or substitutes. *Economics of Education Review, 8*(2), 17-28.

Kapes, J., Mastie, M. M., & Whitefield, E. (1988). *A counselor's guide to career assessment instruments* (2nd ed.). Alexandria, VA: National Career Development Association.

Kendall, E., & Miller, L. (1993, Summer). Attitudes toward school preparation of nontraditional and traditional vocational completers. *Journal of Vocational Education Research, 8*(3), 33-45.

Kostelba, N. (1997). *Variables predicting persistence of community college students.* Unpublished doctoral dissertation, Penn State University, University Park.

Kramer, M. (1998, October). Nutritional lies. *Wine Spectator,* p. 30.

Mohamed, A. (1998). *Participation in vocational education and underemployment among U.S. high school graduates.* Unpublished doctoral dissertation, Penn State University, University Park.

National Center for Education Statistics (NCES). (1990). *NELS 88: First follow-up.* Washington, DC: U.S. Department of Education.

National Center for Education Statistics (NCES). (1992). *NELS 88: Second follow-up.* Washington, DC: U.S. Department of Education.

National Center for Education Statistics (NCES). (1993). *Baccalaureate and beyond: Longitudinal study.* Washington, DC: U.S. Department of Education. (http://nces.ed.gov/surveys/b%26b.html)

National Center for Education Statistics (NCES). (1996). *Student financing of undergraduate education.* NCES #98-076.

National Center for Education Statistics (NCES). (1997, November/ December). Teacher follow-up survey, 1994-95. *Vocational Education Journal,* pp. 22-24.

Noble, B. (1992, November 22). And now the sticky floor. *New York Times.*

Pereira, J. (1997, November 9). The best route to a top college may involve a detour. *Wall Street Journal,* p. 1.

Polls show support for early career preparation. (1998, September 12). *Vocational Training News,* p. 6.

Projections of educational statistics to 2007. (1997, November). *Monthly Labor Review,* pp. 3-5.

Pryor, F., & Schaffer, D. (1997, July). Wages and university education: A paradox resolved. *Monthly Labor Review,* p. 8.

Pucel, D. (1995). Occupation-specific mathematics requirements and application contexts. *Journal of Industrial Teacher Education, 32*(2), 51-75.

Roper Starch Worldwide. (1998, April 23). *Americans want their daughters to be self-reliant, says study by Roper Starch Worldwide* [On-line]. Available: http://biz.yahoo.com/bw/980422/roper_star_1.html

Silvestri, G. (1997, November). Occupational employment projections. *Monthly Labor Review*, pp. 58-83.

Sonoga, C. (1996). Facilitators and barriers to female participation in traditional and nontraditional school-to-work programs. *Occupational Education Forum, 23*(1), 16-24.

Sternberg, L., & Tuchscherer, J. (1992, May). Women in nontraditional careers: Setting them up to succeed. *Vocational Education Journal*, 33-35.

Super, D. (1977). Vocational maturity. *Vocational Guidance Quarterly, 25*(4), 294-304.

Super, D. (1985). *New dimensions in adult vocational and career guidance* (Occasional Paper No. 106). Columbus, OH: National Center for Research in Vocational Education.

Swanson, J., & Miller, E. (1998, April). Technology: Are we helping our daughters? *Tech Directions*, p. 1.

Terrell, K. (1992). Female-male earnings differentials and occupational structure. *International Labor Organizations, 131*(4-5), 387-405.

Tinto, V. (1993). *Leaving college: Rethinking the causes and cures of student attrition* (2nd ed.). Chicago: University of Chicago Press.

Total job openings by education and training. (1997, November). *Monthly Labor Review*, p. 82.

U.S. Department of Commerce, Office of Technology Policy. (1998). America's new deficit. *Update*, pp. 1-3.

U.S. Department of Education, Office of Education Research and Improvement. (1997). *Condition of education* (NCES 97-388). Washington, DC: Author. (www.ed.gov/NCES)

U.S. Department of Labor, Bureau of Labor Statistics. (1998a, January). [On-line]. Available: http://stats.bls.gov/cpsaatab.htm

U.S. Department of Labor, Bureau of Labor Statistics. (1998b, May). *College enrollment and work activity of high school graduates* [On-line]. Available: http://stats.bls.gov/newrels.htm

Wall, J., Passmore, D., et al. (1996). *Community cost of technical skills deficits: A Pennsylvania case study*. University Park: Pennsylvania State University, Workforce Education and Development Program.

Way, W., & Rossman, M. (1996). Family contributions to adolescent readiness for school-to-work transition. *Journal of Vocational Education Research, 21*(2), 5-36.

West Virginia proposed career cluster and career major. (1998). Charleston, WV: West Virginia Department of Education.

Index